Bound to Belém

BOUND to BELÉM

Essays, Poems, Proverbs, Films,
Translations, Travelers' Tales,
Graphics, and Photographs
Brought Back from Brazil

by

James Bogan

MISSOURI PARTNERS PUBLISHING

Missouri Partners Publishing
229 Gentry Hall
Columbia, Missouri, 65201
http://web.mst.edu/~mo-para/

Copyright by James Bogan, 2011
ISBN 978-0-9795643-2-1

All rights, including electronic rights, are reserved. No part of this book may be reproduced or transmitted by any means without the written permission of James Bogan or the publisher, except for brief passages quoted in reviews or scholarly articles.

The author would like to thank the editors of the magazines who have previously published the following poems, essays, and translations:

"The Boat to Bacarena," *North Dakota Quarterly;* "What I Like About Brazil I-II," *Lasting Links: U.S.-Brazil University Partnerships*; "The Street of Thieves," *Walking Magazine;* "T-Shirt Cantata," *Legacy Viewsletter;* "This Ain't the Ozarks Anymore," *Ozark Mountaineer*; "Nightmare in Belém" and "Metamorphoses," *Natural Bridge*; "Twilight Blue, Deleterious," *Tellus;* "Madrugada," *O Liberal*; "What Is the Mystery of Poetry?" *The Stiffest of the Corpse: An Exquisite Corpse Reader*; "Reincarnation," "An Ideogram for Blake," *Latin American Literary Review*; "After completion," *Five Fingers Review*; "Isto por aquilo," *Southwinds*; "Hammock Variations," "The Perils of Poetic Film Making," "Poema Invisivel," "A Quatrain of Improbabilities," "This for That," "To Shan-hui," *New Letters;* "Sad Anthony," "Mar-ahu," "Canticle of the Hammock," *River Styx*.

What I Like About Brazil (I)

All I did was ask for the time of day:
        "Que horas são por favor?"

The fellow I tagged from out the crowd
drew himself up in a full stop
held his ancient silver watch to the sun
and spoke in a musical tone matched to the gentlest look:
        "Quarto horas, quinze minutos, companheiro."

    The warmth of old companions
        kindled between us
            before we resumed
                opposite directions.

DEDICATION

To three of the *Gente Finissima* of Belém do Pará:

Diógenes Leal—Cinematographer, Body Guard, and Pal

Maria Jose Moura e Melo—Brazilian Sister and Counselor

Walkyria Magno e Silva—Student, Translator, and Colleague

CONTENTS

Overture
Getting to Get There Is Half the Fun
High Noon on the Equator
Screenplay #3 for *T-Shirt Cantata*
The Boat to Bacarena
Three Views Around Ver-O-Peso
Hammock Variations
Remembering Max Martins
Selections from the Notebooks of Max Martins
A Batch of Poems by Max Martins
Sights Along the Amazon
In Search of the Rare If Not Non-existent
 Blue Alligator of the Amazon
The Perils of Poetic Filmmaking
Screenplay: *The Adventures of the Amazon Queen*
Two Screenings
Poems from the Streets of Belém
Trance Arrows
Street of Thieves
Beyond Turvania
Four More Poems
Beyond Upper Paradise
Inside Belém
Acknowlegements
Bio-blurb

OVERTURE

"How would you like to teach in Brazil?" This fateful question out of the blue was asked by Eunice French after an Art Appreciation class on old Brueghel I taught in January of 1985. This non-traditional student ran the International Program at the University of Missouri-Rolla.

"Sure," was the immediate response, "but I don't speak a word of Portuguese."

"Not a problem," she claimed. "Give me the ten bucks which will get you enrolled in the Missouri-Pará Partners of the Americas." I did and a month later I was studying *Portuguese for Morons* on a Varig flight from Miami to Belém do Pará. Soon I was happily floundering in the murky river of Amazonian culture, attempting to speak Brazilian Portuguese.

The stories, poems, translations, films, and photographs born of my ongoing experience of Brazil are the substance of *BOUND TO BELÉM.* I was a child in the language then, but made it 1000 miles up the Amazon on "Tudo Bem?" (How are you? /Fine). My first complete sentence: "Onde esta a cerveja? (Where is the beer?), propelled me into the culture. Twenty-six years later, with a cumulative three years of my life spent in Brazil, maybe I am a teenager in the language, relatively fearless and a bit dim, wandering into situations where angels fear to stroll. For example, in 1992 I had gotten myself elected President of the Missouri Partners and was on an official visit, which included an excursion to Das Clinicas, one the good hospitals in Belém. The inspection was arranged by Nazaré Nascimento, a classy lady of a certain age, who had been to Rolla on an exchange the year before. My tour included conversations with bedridden patients, a look into the x-ray room, and a therapeutic art session in the psycho-ward where my own glyph-doodles vibrated congenially amongst their visualizations of interior chaos.

Afterwards there was a formal, but pleasant, luncheon with Nazaré's boss, her colleagues, and two of her doctor sons in attendance. By that time I could blast away in Portuguese, entering sentences whose completion was a matter of improvisation and mangled grammar. Brazilians are given to decorous speeches and I had some experience in this 19th century exercise. Once at a Rotary Club meeting in Belém on Mother's Day I managed to praise everyone's mother including my own, without insulting anyone.

Now some comments were expected as I was wearing an official hat. After the course of fish—*pirarucu*—and before the ice cream—*maracujá*, I stood in front of thirty professionals and bragged on the cleanliness of the facility, the competence of the staff, and the art of the inmates. But I really wanted to say something gracious about Nazaré, who had been so thoughtful, including giving me a shirt without wrinkles to wear to the hospital that very day. I launched into a heartfelt encomium. "Nunca encontrei na minha vida uma mulher como Nazaré'." ("In my life I never met a woman like Nazaré.") My limited vocabulary did not include a word for a person of great energy, so in a split second I defaulted to an English cognate: Pistol. Yes, she was a real pistol, which Brazilianized came out: *Pistoleira*: With a dramatic gesture towards her, I said, "Ela é uma grande pistoleira!"

Instead of expected nods of agreement, the audience sort of twisted, some looked down, some looked around. My faux pas was palpable and, slightly panicked, I careened on grabbing words before I could think. The awkward silence must be filled with something: "Uh, nunca vou esquiser, uh, a noite gloriosa ela passou commigo em Missouri!" I was trying to say, "I'll never forget her great visit in Missouri." What I did say was: "I'll never forget the glorious night we spent together in Missouri!" Eyebrows hit hairlines. Her sons were stunned by the purported escapades of their 70 year old mother. Finally—was it three seconds or three hours later?—someone factored in the shortcomings of my Portuguese and laughed. Everyone laughed. I am still laughing—at myself.

Later I found out what I had said—and learned a new word. A vanilla translation of *pistoleira* is "super-bitch." The good news was they all knew Nazaré for a profoundly gentle and upright woman. If there had been a trace of *pistoleira* in Nazaré, my giraffe would not have been quite so amusing. And now I can deploy *pistoleira* quite accurately, as needed.

Mistake by misdirection I have found my ways, headlong down rivers and up tributaries, not to mention translating poems I have yet to understand. Through mistakes and misdirection—by getting lost— I have landed inside of the Amazon among its people, who have made me quite welcome with tolerance, humor, and big plates of *feijao*. I trust *Bound to Belém* will communicate the distilled pleasures and the occasional thorns of my forays into Brazil. *Boa Viagem!*

Brazil in 1985

GETTING TO GET THERE IS HALF THE FUN

How I came by a trip to Brazil with a First Class ticket all the way from Miami to Rio de Janeiro is a complicated story and not this one. The midnight flight departs from the extremity of the international wing and I hike out early to check in. There is a dragon at the gate but I do not recognize her right off because she is dressed smartly in the guise of a helpful airline attendant.

"I'd like a port window, please."

"Sir, you must have a tie to sit in First Class," she simpered.

"I do enjoy the sunrise from 37,000 feet. What?"

"The Pan Am dress code specifically states that First Class passengers must wear a tie," she reiterated snidely.

"There was nothing about that on my ticket. No smoking, please."

"Sir, we will be happy to seat you in economy class," she said unhappily.

"But I'm going to Brazil, Miss. They don't wear ties in Brazil. Even the President doesn't wear a tie in Brazil."

"That's the regulation, sir," she sneered.

"Kindly hold that seat. I'll be back."

My first thought is to buy a tie directly off the neck of an economy passenger. I scan the travel-anxious crowd but the choice runs from Abbott to Costello, which suits neither my suit nor my fancy. So I trek back to the main terminal to prospect for ties, then walk the gamut of airline counters from Avianca to Varig with stops along the way for Grand Cayman, Air Surinam, and PLUMA (Uruguay), but all the stores are closed. I gather airports do not keep late hours like bus stations or bartenders. Departing travelers are usually long gone by nine and those that arrive late are not going to hang around an airport to look for bargains. One place is still open, <u>The Duty Free Shop</u>. This might be my last chance as I only have fifteen minutes to play with. Beyond the thirty-year old Scotch Whiskey and last week's Japanese gizmos there is a rack of ties unencumbered by tax. Here is a dashing one from Christian Dior, blue-green silk ornamented with centaurs. I even like it and I will wear it again someday, perhaps at the Sagitarian birthday party. A pretty Latino girl cures my reverie: "That one is $40."

"Gosh, imagine what it would be with the tax in New York City, probably $55. Well, no thanks." A quick calculation has told me that I can buy five blue-green hammocks for $40 in the Amazon, including tax. The study fabric would be short on silk centaurs, but colorful.

Ten minutes. Someone is dimming the lights of my last hope, the drug store. Maybe I can improvise on a Floridian pennant. I will cut it up in the shape of a tie and tape it to my shirt. Possibly as I have an emergency strip of duct tape affixed to my briefcase. Or I can cut out the dolphin from a blue t-shirt and make it into a bow-tie. Or...Ah...The Chinese Jump Rope. Yes. And... and... yes, the *Praying Hands* "Inspiratrional Bookmark" made from genuine tin will do it. $2.48 total. Paid.

I carry a second-hand Chinese Army knife for survival in the modern world. With its scissor-blade I cut off a two and half foot piece of the red and blue elastic rope from Hunan. The <u>Praying</u> <u>Hands</u> wrap neatly around the strands and presto! An inspirational string-tie. I hope Pan Am is not as strict as my old grammar school, St. Francis Xavier, which disallowed string ties, probably because they were too easy. I do the 600 yard subdued dash back to the gate practicing my entrance line as I dash; "Ah'm heah fo' mah fust class see-ut, Senhority Megera."*

It worked.

*****

On the return trip from São Paulo I wore silk tie I had swapped for my Chinese string tie. Blue with soup strains. Well, I was seated and already started on a glass of hard-earned champagne when I was called to the jetway: "Sir, the Pan Am dress code specifically states that First Class passengers cannot wear blue jeans."

"Kindly hold that seat. I'll be back."

*Megera: Portuguese for "shrew, punctilious bitch"—from *Megaera*—one of the Furies, a *pistoleira* who hovers about Greek mythology.

High Noon on the Equator

equimatinal
day
of equinoctical
night
noon
sight
straight
up
directly
over
my hatless head
90 degrees
that is
the Sun
blazing
round
absolutely
tops—

for the moment

Belém do Pará
March 21, 1985

Diógenes Leal on Avenida Presidente Vargas
Che says: "We gotta stay tough, without losing our tenderness."

Screenplay #3 for *T-SHIRT CANTATA*

One shirt follows another as you walk along the street in:

    Belém
    State of Pará
    Brasil

    Wild West
    Amazon
    Cowboy
    Break the Dance
    Infinite Liberty
    On the Road
    Track of Nobody

    Midnight
    Mother Survivor
    Nasty
    New York Times
    Rolling Stones
    Jungle Baby
    Satisfaction
    Be a Nice Guy
    Reproduce
    Dangerous Tigers
    One Life to Live. Addict.

    Fact Feet?
            No, Fast Feet
    Rivalry of Winter?
            Yes, Rivalry of Winter

And endless invitations across gentle chests:

Oui!
Yes
I'm ready
I'm EASY
Feel it
Upward Mobility
Oi!
Match 'em up
Imagine
Bottomless
        (not)
            Yours for the Asking

  Garlic Is As Good As Ten Mothers

I'm Nobody
Vote for Jesus
Real Savage
Take Anyone
Mystery
Merda
No Comets

headsonmovingbodiesswingingtotherocksongsthat'sliberty

Charlie Chaplin
Janis Joplin
John Lennon
James Dean
Che Guevara
Charlie
Chaplin

"More than machinery we need humanity."
                                      Charlie Chaplin

And this from the Walt Whitman of Brazil,
Carlos Drummond de Andrade:

The song	Eu preparo
I make	uma canção
will wake	que faça
up	acordar
the old guys	os homens
and bring sleep	e adormecer
to the children	as crianças.

FIM

Note: The t-shirt is the garment of choice in the equatorial city of Belém. *T-Shirt Cantata* began as a list that turned poem, and eventually became a 12 minute documentary film starring the amazing BRANCO, as "The Artist." The soundtrack features authentic music of the Amazon region from the Marapanim Band, Mestre Lucindo and the Canaries, and Adamor do Bandolim.

THE BOAT TO BACARENA

Good luck of sorts directed my way to the boat for Bacarena, though some rationalists might define it a mistake, not in the program at all. I was poking around the *Ver-o-Peso*, the "Check the Weight for Yourself" market in the harbor of Belém. Fast-talking fishmongers hold up whiskery catfish by pink gills to entice buyers from the crowd passing by: "Here's the fresh fellow for your soup cauldron tonight, Senhora!" Row upon row of red, green, yellow, and brown fruits that never show up at Krogers are rainbow-arrayed on long trestle tables. That is not a stubby football, but *cupuaçu* whose juice tastes something like coconut, something like yoghurt, something like *cupuaçu*. I wander among the crammed stalls that display embroidered dresses, leather goods, and lottery tickets, among thousands of other items including live armadillos. Almost everyone wears t-shirts here and the choice at the stands is a varied as the species of fish in the

Amazon. Among the colorful lots of parrots and various representation of Charlie Chaplin are many shirts with their messages in English:

> Bad Boys' Athletic
> Cry in the Night
> Jean Paul Sartre Prep School

The wearers of these body-bulletins frequently do not know what they are broadcasting across their chests. Certainly the ingenuous schoolgirl in the green tie-dyed t-shirt is not NASTY.

Long strings of braided garlic festoon the canvas-draped stalls of the herbalists. I ask a young fellow whose name gets to be Antônio what is the purpose of the six inch stick next to the swordfish beak. "Shave the bark into a glass of water. Let it sit over night. Boil in the morning and before you eat, drink it down with honey and faith—always with faith—and the evil in your back will be banished." Sold.

Who is this? "Santo Antônio." Somebody's hand carved him out of a one inch block of wood and painted the figure from red pedestal to tan tonsured pate. A gold sash encircles his brown robe. The two dots are the eyes of the Christ-child in his arms. What good is St. Antônio? "Ah, Senhor, along with a little faith, Santo Antônio will recover the missing wallet, forgotten promises, and even *almas perdidas* (i.e. lost souls). Also he will match you up with friendly girls." I take six. Next I am introduced to *Caboclo*, the grey house-lizard on a white string leash. His name means something between "medicine man" and "country bumpkin." The tiny woman with the huge gold hoop earrings is Antônio's mother, Elsa. Sweet dark eyes shine from her brown face. Her t-shirt sparkles: "Midnight" from a purple background. She holds up a jar of bona-fide home-made snake oil. How do I know it is snake oil? Because I can see the small viper nestled dead amongst herbs and flowers, pickled in alcohol. "Smell it," she says. I do. Much closer to Chanel #5 than Jungle Gardenia. She spreads some on my arm. What is it for? "Great good luck." I take two ounces which she pours through a small funnel into a heart-shaped bottle. Anointed for good fortune, I set out to seek it.

The sun is directly overhead, so it must be noon here two degrees south of the equator but the temperature is no worse than

a Missouri day in August. Less humid, too. Still I would like a cold beer and a bit of shade. About a mile across the river lies an island that looks ideal for an "Antarctica" and a palm tree to drink it under. All I have to do is get from here to there on one of the half-dozen ferry boats moored by the market, but which one? The deck hand from the *Jarau* stands ready to cast off so I ask him where he is bound as I point hopefully across the bay. Are you going over there? "Baracena?" he replies. Over there, I say. "Bacarena." He says. OK. It is going to cost 5000 cruzeiros, about one American dollar. Seems a little steep compared to an eight-cent bus. Still, it's a bargain and I jump aboard, joining a semi-circle of one girl and seven men who are waiting for the pilot and the deck hand to crank the engine up. Literally. The diesel is mulish and the two men work in feverish tandem to set it off. Finally it catches and we chug away into the brown waters of Guaraja Bay headed for Bacarena.

The unity of the river succeeds the multiplicity of the market. The broad expanse of tropical sky covers green islands, sundazzled bay, and receding city. An inbound freighter pierces the eastern horizon which is still a hundred miles to the ocean. The *Jarau* passes under the stern of a rusting grey freighter that points upstream, tugging at the anchor chain. The river current swirls along its water-line. One of our passengers, a toothless old guy, dips a tin can into the river and drinks it down. My eyes pop at the sight. After all the warnings I have heard about the ravaging effects of untreated water, I watch out the corner of my eye to see if he will be devoured from the inside out by microbes. I would not make it past Monday if I drank that mix. He smiles a satisfied smile; and since he is not dead already, I conclude his immune system is in the avant garde of human evolution.

As we near the shore, a channel opens to the interior of the island and no doubt the dock at Bacarena. Gliding along the palm-lined jungle passage, I feel like I am aboard the *African Queen*, make that the *Amazon Queen*. In fifteen minutes we have journeyed from metropolis to jungle, *floresta* in Portuguese, and it is a forest of blossoms and trees with dozens of green birds flitting about and batches of blue butterflies each one big as a hat. No lie.

A dark fellow with dark eyes motions for me to follow him and I do, trusting his Charlie Chaplin t-shirt straightaway. He climbs along the gunwale and then hoists himself up to the roof of the little boat. We stretch out on the impromptu sundeck and I find out Mario is on his way to work in an oil refinery two boat transfers upriver. His six month New Jersey English is better than my barbaric Portuguese. I keep my eyes peeled for Bacarena which has to be around the next bend... or the next. I ask Mario when will we get to Bacarena, is there a beach, and can we get a beer? "Soon. No. Yes."

Occasionally we steam by a thatched shack with a long wooden canoe tied up at a plank pier in front. Snakefish, the size of green crayons, leap across the surface of the water. Giant samaumeira trees, the sycamore of the Amazon, outreach the palms. A phalanx of yellow birds crosses our bow. More butterflies. A kingfisher! is the first familiar bird I have seen. Its animated chatter sounds like the same dialect used by cousins 8000 miles nearer the North Pole. The boat comes out the other side of the island into a major channel of the river and in sight of more islands. "There are thousands of islands, my friend, and most of them are nameless."

Where's Bacarena anyway? Mario goes to ask the pilot, and the answer he comes back with releases me from the anticipation of the next bend: "Nobody up there is quite sure, but certainly we will make Bacarena by dark." So, that is that and glad to be here, rounding the point of another forested nameless island. Ah, the joys of misadventuring and plenty of time to get there in. All preconceptions overboard! I am in the hands of the pilot Miguel and my own ignorance, happily sprung out of all programming. Each moment now is a gift of misdirection

> Clouds pile up and disperse.
> The fine rain comes and goes.
> Horizontal meditation shifts into sleep.

And out again to find myself invited by Miguel to take the wheel. Calling on the skills developed in my youth as a Chicago cab driver and my maturity as an all-weather Ozark canoeist, I walk forward to pilot this little craft on the world's mightiest river system. The rest of the passengers eye me with a mixture of envy and amusement as I sit down on the plank seat behind the wheel which was probably scavenged from a '49 Hudson. Two frayed blue nylon lines run through pulleys to the rudder astern. Boats going downstream just head for the middle of the river and get a continual boost from the current. But we are headed upstream and the trick is to stay as close to shore as possible—without running aground or hitting a snag. I watch carefully for telltale turbulence that might signal a sunken limb. At the first suspicious swirl, I turn the wheel sharply only to discover more play than in a six-month spaniel. The *Jarau* flattens this phantom swirl. Miguel takes a nap anyway. For the next hour I scan the shore, stick to the bank, measure channel crossings, and make my turns long before necessary so they happen just in time. Sam Clemens would have appreciated this opportunity and known what to do with it too. Finally the white buildings of Bacarena appear. Miguel reassumes his post and docks the boat deftly at a rickety pier. Mario and I debark shouting "*Boa Viagem!*" as we go.

The jungle edges the town of broad streets that are filled more with strolling couples and kids riding double on bicycles than motored vehicles. Our destination now is the home of a friend of Mario's who turns out to be a dead ringer for Hailie Selassie and is cordial as a king. We sit in his front yard listening to the loud music from the bar across the street. The long sought "Antartica" arrives and some crabmeat on a stick that far outclasses any corndogs in my experience. The afternoon wanes in pleasant idleness. The town's people promenade. Black buzzards sometimes soar overhead.

On our return to the port we detour along a jungle path where I meet my first *seringueira* tree. Ancient scars mark the bark where milky juice had been collected to make rubber at the cost of seven Indian lives per ton, roughly figured.

At the dock Mario flags down another small ferry bound for Belém and sees me securely aboard before he goes off to find his own boat headed upriver. Soon we are moving swiftly with the current, sundown at our stern. The pilot, a strong old man, tells me about the dangers of making this trip in fog. He switches on a spot light and makes the sign of the cross to demonstrate his two prime tools for confronting obscurity. But this night is clear. Orion, who I am used to seeing at forty-five degrees, stalks the zenith at this latitude. Yes, the earth <u>is</u> round! The rest of the trip unfolds as a dark dream of jungle sounds with a continual diesel bass. The Southern Cross stands just above the black tree line. Eventually the channel opens to the bay and the million white lights of Belém brighten the eastern horizon. Santo Antônio, snake-oil, and a little bit of faith has seen me through.

THREE VIEWS AROUND VER-O-PESO
by Branco Medeiros

HAMMOCK VARIATIONS

AN ESSAY, POEMS, PROVERBS, TRAVELERS' TALES AND A FILM ABOUT GOD'S OWN BED

Habit blinds us to what our eyes see day-in-day-out. How often do we admire the common objects around us? Do we ever dream of discovering their origins?

Cicero
De Natura Deorum, II-xxxviii

Advisory for the Ideal Reader:

Before attempting to read this essay, find a hammock and get in it, as there is simply no better place to read.

*****

"Old Mother." That is what denizens of the Amazon call their hammocks. As in our first unremembered memories, *mãe velha* enfolds us in comforting arms, besides protecting us from scorpions, mists, and serpents that meander along the ground. The infant, born in the jungle by the shore of a river, sleeps his first sleep in the hammock, as his grandfather will sleep his last. Then, as is our simple custom, we bury the old man in his own hammock. We are born, we live, we love, we die in the hammock, and then our friends carry us to the boneyard in *mãe velha* to rest up till Judgment Day.[1]

How often can scholars cite the first day a word entered a language? In 1500 on the 27th of April, a Friday, the Portuguese explorer Pero Vaz de Caminha walked along a sandy beach in Brazil and on that rainy day noted in his journal: "In their thatched houses the natives sleep in NETS that are attached with cords to the wooden beams above. Below always burns a small fire to keep them warm and to repel bugs and demons." He saw an Indian dozing comfortably in what looked like a fishing net, and so from that day the Portuguese expression for hammock is *rede de dormir*: "a net for sleeping." In English, the word "hammock" came by way of Spanish conquistadors, who derived the word *hommoca* from the Caribs, who wove fibers of their hammok trees into nets for sleeping. The ferocious Caribs learned the craft from a people they had conquered, the inventive, but more peaceable, Arawak tribe whose own word for "hammock"—*ini*—translates as: "bed-threads."

NEW WORLD HAMMOCK HISTORY

In 1570 Pero de Magalhães testifies to the total absorption of the hammock into the life of European colonials: "Most of the beds in Brazil are hammocks, hung in the house from two cords. This custom they took from the Indians of the land."

***

In 1600, a hundred years after Pero Vaz de Caminha first slept in a hammock, Jean de Lery wrote: "Whenever we entered a village, according to the custom of the land, we sat each one of us in a hammock."

***

It is not without a moment of tenderness, as Camara Cascudo noted in his hammock classic *Rede de Dormir*, that we record the intrepid Alexander Von Humboldt slept in a hammock and woke to hear the voice of a parrot in the jungle of the Orinoco. It was the year 1800. In its youth this ancient parrot had lived with the Atures tribe who had died off in the wilderness in terrorized flight from the Caribs. This parrot talked their language. His was the last voice of the extinguished Atures heard along the Orinoco.

***

By the 18th century conquistadors had naturalized into the marauding born-in-Brazil *bandeirantes,* who slept in hammocks. Missionaries slept in hammocks. Plenty of wayward adventurers starved in hammocks. In 1915 Teddy Roosevelt slept in a hammock along the Rio da Dúvida, caught malaria, and survived long enough to hear that the river he explored was re-named after him, before he died.

***

"I have many occasions to notice that everywhere there were Indians, the Europeans have destroyed them, but first they appropriated their customs, like paddling their canoes, eating their potatoes and tomatoes, smoking their tobacco, growing their corn, and sleeping in their hammocks."

>Augusto de Sainte-Hilairez—1822

***

Sell everything, if you have to, but hold on to your hammock.

Whoever has a hammock, lies in it.
>Whoever lacks it, looks for it.

You don't have to be "Super-Swami" to levitate in a hammock.

THERE ARE MANY REASONS WHY THE HAMMOCK BEATS THE BED

We have to fit ourselves to the grid of a bed,
    but the hammock molds itself to our forms.

The bed, hardly a fellow traveler of our desires,
        squares off sleep;
but the hammock collaborates
    in the movement of our dreams.

Now the bed requires us to take its manner,
    fixing us to itself,
    and we look for repose
    in a succession of positions;
but the hammock takes on our individual shape
    and becomes one with our habits,
    answering individual form.

The bed is rigid, predetermined, and angular;
but the hammock is hospitable, comprehensive,
    and accommodating,
    ready to meet all the whims of our fatigue
    and the unforeseen containment of our tranquility.

    The old mother and the young wife.

When we find our spot in a hammock, our bodies correspond with ancestors beyond memory. Gravitationally inevitable, this congruence stretches back before the Fall, as Adam only took to his bed after the expulsion from Eden.

First cousin of the fisherman's net, the hammock holds our bodies and catches our dreams. Do you suppose the spider's web was its aboriginal inspiration, sometime back in the early Paleolithic?

The hammock is suspect in societies where King Clock determines behavior, because the hammock annihilates time. Hours do not apply. Think more in terms measured by sun and moon rather than the decimauled seconds of modern "chronometers." Afternoon, evening, night, morning are the human portions of the day—any one of which can be fulfilled in the hammock. The true enemy of hurry and foe of habitual agitation defeats all those demands for constant change of scene. Even though the hammock was born in a primeval culture, it still soothes a body rattled in the 21st century by reconciling the fundamental contraries of movement and stillness.

The hammock ranks with the wheel and the centerboard for enhancing life and trade. What benefactor to humanity asks so little in return? Can your car compare?

And what would sailors have done without hammocks? Bunks, that's what they did, until Portuguese and Spanish mariners introduced this old New World invention to India, China, and all navies European and American. The Chinese may have invented everything from the five dollar bill to fireworks, but the honor of a net for sleeping belongs to tropical America.

Figure a good bed costs   the cradle
  a month of toil   outperforms
    but the hammock takes   and finally
      only a day's labor   into a suitcase
        then doubles   rolls
            as a chair   into a couch
                stretches

CANTICLE OF THE HAMMOCK

On the old plantations in the lands of the North
that's where you would find pretty hammocks
with intricate fringes the color of the moon...
I remember my grandfather, remembering the girls of Recife.
I can see him still, stretched out in the hammock
his large feet bare, his head turned to the past.

And I remember his mother,
Sonia, she was a little oldie,
seated in the hammock, talking alone
with eyes full of shades from beyond.
Actually she was a poor thing,
perched in the hammock
that comes and goes
vaivem vaivem
that comes and goes

In the shacks by the road
in the palaces of the rich
innocent children swing in the hammock.
A mother lulls the swaying child
with songs smooth, soft, and gentle.
She imagines these songs sung
by birds in the kingdom of Heaven.

Even on a long road comes sweet rest
for soldiers of the infantry.
Then they lay in their grey hammocks
reposed after the long day's march
suspended amongst the crowded trees
watching the stars, lost in the sky.

And is not the hammock a proper vessel for the dead?
The dead one looks asleep
dreaming a dream of emptiness
echoing with the cries of the living.
Carried by two friends
the body rocks to the rhythm of their walk.
Carried by two friends
the body swings until it comes to rest
in the depths of the ground.

Ah, the new moon is a silver hammock
shining in our sky suspended on the deep.
"God rests in this moon," old Sonia says.
Does He rest in the beautiful floating moon
watching from afar the sorrows of his distant children?

R. Friere Ribeiro[2]

MACUNAÍMA SAYS...

Macunaíma, the dubious doyen of Brazilian culture, says:

There are certain things of this world that really
    give a guy grief, like:

        Riding an unruly burro
            Writing with a pen that scrapes
                Or digging a splinter out with a dull knife.

    But worst of all is to find yourself
        taking a siesta in a house without shade
            wrapped in a sheet that's too short
                condemned to a ripped hammock--
            slashed of its grace,
                    breached of its balance.

DIRECTIONS

How few people know the real comfort of a hammock! A hammock ought to be hung from sturdy hooks about six feet from the ground and about ten feet apart, preferably slung between two shady trees. Here's a familiar enough sight and a pleasant dream: The hammock on the beach swaying with the breeze, shaded by coconut palms.

The hammock should NOT be stretched out horizontal, like the flight deck of an aircraft carrier. The well slung hammock resonates to the curve of the sliver moon and hovers so low that you can touch the earth with your hand, pick up a book, a cold beer. In the case of unforeseen disaster, there is not far to fall. A Euclidean secret is to position yourself at a forty-five degree angle and your body will flatten out most comfortably. If you end up in the shape of a human banana, you are not corresponding properly with the ancestors.

In the hammock the occupant can converse, sell stuff, make plans, form alliances, reconcile opposites, discourse, propose, and dispose. As an enhancement to sexual play, the hammock is a prodigious, but sometimes unpredictable, force. And there's more: outright relaxing, sleeping, dozing, napping. Try playing back-gammon in a hammock with a relative. Or imitate, if you dare, some hammock-floating "colonel" after dinner: smoking a cigar, fanning himself, spitting on the floor, belching loud as a Sultan, picking off nits, scratching feet and balls.

*****

Stow the crybaby in a deep hammock.

Sleep in a torn hammock, wake up on the floor.

The devil chose hell over a thoughtful hammock.

LOST AND FOUND

The other night I walked the beat
pacing like a rat behind a wall
I looked and looked
for the slanted ropes
of your sweet hammock
but I couldn't find you

Last night I had a dream--
Oh my God, what an impudent dream!
I dreamt us in my hammock
and I held you in the shape of your clothes
It was you in the the shape of your clothes

                            Feliciano Gonçalves Simões

*****

What is the only real problem with a hammock?
                                            Getting out of it.

It comes, it goes--*vaivem vaivem*.
The oscillation of the hammock
that old *vaivem*—
annuls the forces of a bad spell.

If you don't know the knot, you are going to know the floor.

*****

QUIZ

What is our cradle, our nuptial bower, our sickbed, our coffin?[4]

ONE DAY IN THE POETIC DOCUMENTARY FILM TRADE

"*Eigendynamik ist Zauber*," said Max Plank, one inebriated night in dark Berlin. "Momentum is Magic." Anyway, my oft-touted idea to make a film about hammocks was a reality again. I had shot an hour's worth of hammock vendors, hammock weavers, and hammock dwellers in 1990 and here I was three years later with 100 minutes of virgin 16mm film to expose to the equatorial sun. The hammock is colorful, folkloric, comfortable, cool, portable and an ideal subject for prolonged research. Having been two degrees south of the equator before, I had spent a lot of time just suspended in the hammock in a relentless effort to keep my body rested in the draining heat and humidity. Besides, I loved the sense of instant levitation available readily to the most inept beginner.

Following the leads of local friendship, my crew had ended up in the ancient fishing village of Itapuá. Itapuá means "big rock" but I cannot say I saw even a pebble in this sea-level, mud-banked village near Vigia at the entrance to the southernmost channel of the Amazon. A landing of strategic importance long ago, it still has fertile fishing grounds and lots of nets. We are about fifty miles south of the equator. Marajó, an island the size of Switzerland—though not nearly so tall—lies in the Amazon River, just beyond sight over the horizon.

Something there is about a camera accompanied by 16mm color film, wild ideas, and a squad of collaborative artists. "Hammock luck" met us at every turn. We were on our way to the house of Manoel Augosto, the 93-year-old *curandeiro*, known for his skills as a healer of souls as well as a setter of bones. As we rounded a muddy bend, there was a boy in a yard swinging high in his hammock. I said to Cris, our anthropologist-grip, "Can we stop?" So our caravan of two cars did. She asked the family if it would be okay to film and as usual in Brazil it was more than okay. I almost always ask before I film somebody and few Brazilians refuse to gather their spirits and shine for the camera.

I chose an angle for the shot that would show the mud-wall chicken house, the dirt road, and the boy who was soaring in his hammock, one end hooked to an old tree and the other to a snag that wobbled considerably. I told Diógenes, my camera-man-body guard, how I wanted him to start with the top of the shaking tree and tilt down to reveal the boy--and then to shoot whatever else he wanted at his discretion, which was my standard direction: Shoot what I ask for and beyond that get what you can. Radio music blared throughout from nearby houses and a clutch of neighbors viewed our machinations with mild curiosity.

"Roll'em," I say and Diógenes responds with: "*Rodando*" ("Rolling"). The boy in the hammock pushes off with his hand from a board on the ground with every other swing, and the hammock rides an arc of about 220 degrees. His hand on the offbeat slices the air like the prow of a schooner under sail and I catch his eye and answer his smile. He soars.

A kid pulling a squeaky wood truck walks by and I redirect him into the foreground of the scene and we shoot it again. The boy in the hammock was in the kinetic heaven of untrammeled motion. I did not notice his thin tangled limbs. Later in his home I saw how he kept to the floor, with his paralytic legs askew.

While we were filming, Alan, the sound guy-location scout, spotted the boy's sister weaving a fishing net. The blue wooden house was clean and airy and basic with open windows in the front room. The girl, Rosa, had three strands of white twine tied to a window sill and her nimble hands never stopped lacing and knotting and looping the strings into a sturdy net for fishing: *rede de pescar*.[3]

We had to set up the camera in a confined space on the best but heaviest tripod in the world. ("Sell everything if you have to, O Filmmaker, but hold on to your tripod.") Rosa's backlit figure was framed by the window with the tropical vegetation outside. In the foreground are three ceramic chickens on a crocheted doily and knick-knacks, second cousin to those found on the shelves of lace-curtain Irish bungalows on the south side of Chicago. Family pictures are flanked by Jesus, Mary, and St. Anthony.

Rosa worked on silently as we fiddled with the machines and faddled with the light meters. We filmed as she laced, knotted, and looped. Occasionally she would let a cascade of newly knotted net fall from her hand and then she laced, knotted, and looped some more.

Across the dirt street on the corner stood a prototype of the modern convenience store. The few wooden shelves are stocked with penny candy, tins of dried milk, cooking oil, flour, and sugar. A battery operated radio crackles out pop music in competition with a blaring radio on a different channel down the block. The building itself was on classic gabled-roof lines. The walls were dried mud and split bamboo and the roof palm-thatch. The proprietor just happened to be conducting business from a yellow hammock. Let's film.

Diógenes set the camera up at the angle to catch two sides of the simple but impressive building. An amputee on crutches, wearing a straw hat, hobbles up and buttresses himself against the corner of the house. Fine. Two kids jump to the window level, elbows braced on the shelf, feet dangling a foot off the ground. Fine.

It starts to rain steadily. Not fine, but we film anyway because Cris, Iracema, Maria José, and Marcia—friends and schleppers—hold a black tarp over Diógenes who is embracing the camera as he shoots. The women look Brazilian Caryatids—lovely, and sturdy enough to hold the makeshift roof up! It continues to rain. We film the proprietor in his yellow hammock selling some red sugar candies to the two kids at the window shelf-counter. The one-legged man remains propped up at the corner of the store. The rain pours down. *Chuva. Chuva. Chuva.* Cut. Let's get out of here.

Three sequences have multiplied out of the glancing sight of a boy swinging high in a hammock. Hammock luck. Before we go, I hold the hand of the hammock-boy. The proprietor of the shop offers me a gift, a *cupuaçu*, which is the size and shape of a football. The pulp is ever so sweet and tastes like, like *cupuaçu*. Rosa all the while knots, loops, and splices.

We drive along the red dirt road to the last house of the village, a blue cottage with flowers around it. A meadow of tall grass extends to the tree lined horizon. St. Benício is hand-lettered in blue over a Dutch door. We enter a waiting room, equipped with two red benches. As usual in Brazilian domiciles, the floor is well swept. A picture of Jesus hangs next to formal tinted photographs of an old couple. It is Manoel Augusto and his wife--30 years ago. Joel, our grip-cook, had met Manoel when he messed up his leg in an Itapuá soccer game. With inflamed nerves from hip to foot, Joel could hardly walk. The healer wedged a coke bottle behind Joel's knee and then yanked his leg back. Joel nearly put his head through the low roof in response; but the next day his leg was better, and a week later he was playing soccer again.

Manoel Augusto is a bone-setter of long experience. This time Joel has a bunged up toe from a missed shot on goal and I figure as long as I have traveled 10,000 kilometers, the last ten of which have been over a dirt, sometimes mud road, I might as well let him take a crack at my overburdened back. I will try my luck, which is a kind of faith, I guess.

Under his own steam Manuel walks carefully down a narrow corridor into the room. He is nearly blind with cloudy cataracts; his teeth are gone; his skin is several shades of brown and purple: and his nose is recently scuffed to the point of bleeding; but his voice is solid and his force palpable. He is 93, hears well, remembers everything, and is quite up to the job of "representing" his art in front of a group of techno-creatures from the big city of Belém and from the boondocks of Ozarks.

He sits in the low-slung hammock with his feet on the floor. The *curandeiro* is assisted by his wife. She looks most of her seventy-eight years, but her eyes are clear clear clear and there are still strands of black in her long hair. He sits in his hammock and we arrange it as best we can to catch light filtered through a cloudy sky.

Manuel says he will work on the man with the bad back first. I instruct Diógenes not to spend film on my treatment. I look into the wreck of the old man's face, which emanates kindness. He puts his hands on my shoulders. I shut my eyes and keep them shut, trying to let whatever might happen, happen. Floating in darkness, it seems easy enough to believe in his power. He starts with a blessing, a prayer in a musical tone. I thought I was going to get a few chiropractic whacks and twists and that would be that. I can only understand some of the words fleetingly but catch on soon enough that he has diagnosed my back problem. Something about *pedras*— stones—blocking my path and heavy loads, *cargas* on my back.

I have been in his presence for three minutes and he has sized me up intuitively, though I suppose most forty-five year olds would fit the profile. He calls on a batch of Christian and Macumba saints: The Good Jesus, Santa Maria, Iemenjá, and St. Anthony. St. George too. A small statue of that knight on horseback fights a dragon on a tabletop. Given the intractable nature of my problems, Manoel needs to invoke a litany of entities to undo the screwed up circuits in my lower back. (Do I hear the camera running?) His hands lay gently on my shoulder, as he circles around me with a chant of lilting words. I realize I am in the center of a blessing bestowed in Old Testament proportions. I let it wash over me.

Rei Tupi, Rei Tupi	King Tupi, King Tupi
Estou aqui, estou aqui	I am here, I am here
Eu posso conseguir	I will do what I can do

He touches my shoulder softly and occasionally punctuates the petitions with some forceful breathing. His rhetoric is quiet and strong—not the dramatic blather of trained TV preachers. Then I do hear to understand: "From this time forward do not look back. *Não olha atrás*." (Hardline New Age advice that.) "The stones are no longer in your path. The road is clear… Amen." A harsh exhalation. A silence. I open my eyes and thank him. Something had happened.

Then Diógenes frames and films Manoel's beat up face as he works on Joel's gimpy toe and I imagine a sequence towards the end of the *Hammock Variations* with that focused ancient face filling the screen.

((A week later I am a thousand miles up the Araguaia River. I find myself running along a sandy river-beach just for the fun of it. For five years I had not been able to run because of my back. Now, many years further on, I can still run. This may all be anecdotal, but it is my anecdote.))

Joel has found a baby in a hammock. The film needs that baby to counter-balance the old healer and serve as the eventual follow-up to the barely silhouetted lovers disappearing into their hammock. The opening montage will be pinned to rhythmic swinging:

> lovers
>   baby
>   kids
>   teenager
>   adults male
>   adults female
>   ancestor
> all God's chilluns in hammocks

Well, Joel has found a baby in a hammock, so we pack our gear for the short ride to the baby's thatched house. A passel of kids plays out front at a small pool table (*mesa de sinuca*). They lead us through a clutter and clatter of dispersing chickens and through a lean-to kitchen at back. Everything is well swept and orderly. One little girl fans the charcoal fire with a woven palm fan. In the bedroom four hammocks in tiers hang under an open pediment of light at the roofline. An infant, pacifier in mouth and white cap on head, sways in a small hammock. The mother on a bed beneath looks fairly exhausted. What are WE doing here? The fisherman-father has said okay, but I ask her directly and she agrees on her weary own. And the light is too dim. Can we move the baby's hammock? Okay.

Now the light is right. The smoke from the charcoal fire has dissipated and somebody has swiped the pacifier from the baby who is black haired and content in the hammock. The

baby does not mind our presence, seems curious in a nine-day-old way. The mother rests easily amongst the cinematic hubbub. We film the straw walls in straw-filtered light and the baby
> in a hammock, peaceful as Jesus in the stable.

"How old is your baby?"

"Nine days old."

"Brand new! What's his name? What's her name?"

I get a quizzical look.

"*Nené*." Baby. Generic baby.

Later on Cris explains that the families around here often do not name the baby until after the fourth month. This *nené* seems fairly healthy, I say. "It's after the first month that things go wrong."

All the above happened within twenty four hours, not to mention but mentioning just the same: yielding the road to an elephantine water buffalo with its convoluted horns pulling a cart named *Esperança*--"Hope"; and finally, Venus looms big as a basketball in the *madrugada*, the hour before dawn.

*****

> The one who knows how to string up a hammock
> > can maintain it.

> If you don't love your hammock,
> > you just don't know how to love.

> As the old timer said to the clerk at a hotel without hooks
> > for his hammock:
> > > "Sonny, I ain't sick enough to sleep in a bed."

IN A HAMMOCK

Of course I feel like a child
when I swing in a hammock
That sweet oscillation puts me in mind
of songs low and soft
I heard as a child half-sleeping
on my mother's breast

And now there's my hammock
Gentle in its ever ready welcome
This dream friend suits my taste
and from my body takes its form
and turns itself to my pleasure
and my body in turn
answers all the entreaties of the wind

The hammock gestures in the nuance of hesitation:
retreat and advance—
It comes and goes in the old *vaivem*
of its swaying this way and that

Such a wide and sufficient trance
induced by the hammock leaves the body fluid,
now dreaming itself into the langorous arms
of a palpable dream lover
launched on a Sea of Tranquility.
I navigate waves of air
towards a country called Chimera
where an uncertain someone
— someone I live to desire—
beckons me and waits for me

Gilka Machado

THE POSTSCRIPT

In the next several weeks we shot up all the negative I had hand-carried around numerous x-ray machines from the shores of the Missouri River to the banks of the Amazon. Ten reels—one hundred minutes of 16mm Kodak 7292 film stock. We filmed at the docks, on ships, in honking city plazas, young and old and in between, male and female did we shoot them. We shot at dawn. We shot in the dark: "That's not going to work!" And it didn't. We shot it all up.

Then I departed Pará for the central-highlands state of Goiás where a week long canoe voyage down the Rio Araguaia was my reward for six weeks of filming, taping, and talking. I really wanted to escape the tyranny of cameras and let my eyes focus without ulterior motives, and I needed to get my Portuguese river vocabulary functional. It was a glorious trip of days---fast floating (*flutuando*) down the wide brown river, crossing in the current (*correnteza*) from side to side, and spooking hundreds of herons (*garças*) and dozens of small alligators (*jacaré*). My favorite Ozark bird is the King Fisher, who has a common cousin here: *Martin Pescador*--Martin the Fisherman.

Of course, each night I slung my hammock and dozed and dreamt and slept under southern constellations. How southern? Well, we had the Southern Cross in view, and to engage in a bit of hemispheric-centrism, I will claim that it does not really equal its less famous, but more spectacular opposite number: the Northern Cross, which also goes by the name of Cygnus, the Swan. Just after sunset, the Big Dipper appears, emptying itself just over the horizon. The two pointer-stars aim DOWN towards the implied Polaris, out of sight on the other side of the heavens, probably.

Fate confirmed my hammock researches on the banks of the Araguaia. The village of Cochalin lay on the Mato Grosso side of the river and we lingered at the ferry landing on the Goiás side under a shady roof and drank cold beer and ate fresh caught and soon fried fish. We had just packed up two canoes and four guys worth of gear onto and into a car the size of an old Nova. Compact, but at least not sub-compact. Given the prospect of a seven hour ride back to the big city with the first 100 kilometers on red dirt roads, we ordered another round of fish and beers to forestall the inevitable insertion of five guys into the already overloaded car.

The ferry-barge has just brought a canvas-draped truck across the river and a short fellow hops out of the back and comes over to sell me the blue hammocks draped over his shoulder. Six store-bought hammocks are already stowed in my bag back in the city, ready for export. Still, this fellow—"My name is Ignacio, from Recife"—has some pretty hammocks, and it is such a pleasure to be hammock-rich and I like him, so, what the hell; I buy two comfortable ones for a twenty dollar bill. I follow him back to his truck, as he wants to introduce me to his work mates. They are slotted three high and six deep in hammocks slung in the back of the truck. A golden light filters through the canvas. Smiles emanate from the gang of itinerant Nordestino *rede*-salesmen, two days into a five day journey back home to Recife for a month off. They expect to be in Goiânia tonight. Yes, I expect to be in Goiânia tonight too.

So I ask Ignacio if his boss would give me a ride—*uma carona*—to the capital. I have a brand new hammock I would like to try out. In a moment he returns with a big smile and, it seems, I have been accepted into the Guild of Hammock Vendors. It takes about three minutes to explain to my companions what is up. They are amazed and delighted to be rid of me.

Ignacio ties my hammock into slot 1A, at the front on the lowest level. He has rescued me from a spot more cramped than a middle airplane seat (37D) and put me in a first class luxurious hammock-recliner with a great view plus ventilation. Directly above me hovers Joãozinho and to my left swings a bearded Francisco, who looks like the innocent twin of Chuck Knapp, the engineer at the Public Radio station back home. With a bit of jostling I stretch my feet out behind Francisco's neck.

A round of greetings all the way back to Row 6, Slot C, comes my way: "*Tudo bem*!" The hammocks sway in rhythm to the undulations of the red dirt road. I am in purple-patterned Hammock Heaven. After three months in the interior, they have sold two thousand hammocks among them. Zacharias, a boy of seventeen, is younger than my son Jesse and has already been on the hammock road full time for three years. He can read, but his compatriot, Fernando, cannot. We talk about five-minute-a-day lessons. Once again I am amazed at the instant *amizade*—friendship—that seems the rule of my Brazilian experience. I tell them the exotic story about my father to the north who lives on Mackinac Island where there are no cars, few hammocks, and lots of ice. Ignacio tells me about his family with two boys back in Pernambuco. Three months work, minus room and board (read: truck and rice) has yielded about $350. He says his boss is a reasonable type, but somehow I doubt if there is a medical plan in his unwritten contract.

Now the gentle heat and road-drone makes me sleepy, as broad stretches of hilly Goiás curve by. For the next five hours I am in a trance. The truck is jammed but comfortable. (As my mother says, "In confined spaces, good manners prevent murder.") Behold the sliver moon, looking like a silver hammock in the sky, accompanying us across the sky as we rumble down the road. I can bend my head outside to catch the red sunset and the brewing rainclouds that extinguished it. Fernando pulls a yellow tarp out of a storage compartment and seals us inside, just before rattling rain pummels the truck. Now it seems we could be anywhere and in the dark the eighteen hammocks still sway and still I dream a dream of rimed motion: I am sailing on Lake Huron, a green swell lifts me smoothly up and settles me smoothly down.

Grinding gears shatter my fragile maritime reverie, as we come to a stop at a roadside café. Great logistical good fortune! My canoe-compatriots arrive within the minute. I roll up my goods into my new hammock and cram it into the cramped car. Ignacio accepts a couple of twenties which will get presents for his kids and beers for our companions. I make a verbose farewell, worthy of a Rotarian, to my suspended friends. Ignacio and I embrace, and then I stand waving in a black cloud of diesel as they head off East for Recife. How is it that after weeks of hammock "research" and filming, I should be picked up by a truckload of hammock vendors hours from the nearest no place and taken in as one of their own?

THE POET AND THE WEAVER
AND THE WEAVER
AND THE POEM

The weaver weaves her threads
to catch our bodies.
The poet turns his lines
to catch our souls.
It is a joy to take the hammock off the loom
It is a sorrow to string the loom anew
The weaver weaves
thread by thread
as the shuttle flies
one side to the other
thread turns on thread
one side to the other
even as the poet
forms words out of words

The weaver weaves her threads.
The poet fills his lines with sound
till the poem becomes a vessel
to hold breath
inspiration by expiration.
We live out our days
line by line,
thread by thread
we weave our lives.

The weaver dreams in the hammock
she has brought forth from the loom.
She dreams of the poet dreaming in turn...

Suspended in the hammock
he floats between earth and sky:
the hammock sports a lacey fringe
and hangs on hooks
between life and death .
And it is best to forget all the bad.
And it is best to forget all the good.
A thought comes, a thought goes.
Vaivem. Vaivem.

*****

SOME NOTES

[1] Parts of this piece are re-drawn from Luis da Camara Cascudo's fabulous book about hammocks, *Rede-de-Dormir*, originally published by the Ministério da Educação e Cultura Serviço de Documentação in Rio de Janeiro (1959). The translations of the prose, and especially the poetry, which Cascudo anthologized in his book, are of a free nature. Hopefully the spirit of the Portuguese carries through in its English vessel.

[2] Here is what the "Canticle of the Hammock," written by F. Friere Ribeiro in 1957, looks like in the original:

CÂNTICO EM LOUVOR DA REDE-DE-DORMIR

>Nos velhos engenhos,
>nos grandes sobrados
>das terras do norte,
>as redes bonitas
>de lindas varandas
>da cor do luar!...
>Recordo o passado:
>meu avô, homen feito,
>formado em Direito,
>lembrando o Recife
>deitado na rede
>de papo-pro-ar!
>
>Sinhazinha, velhinha,
>sentada na rede, falando sozinha
>com os olhos tão cheios
>das sombras do além.
>Sinhazinha, coitada,
>na rede deitada,

na rede que vai,
que vai e que vem!

Nas longas estradas,
nas doce paradas,
deitados nas redes
descansam tropeiros
das grandes jornadas,
nas árvores belas,
olhando as estrelas
perdidas no ceu

Nos lares humildes,
na casa dos ricos
as redes balançam
inocentes meninos.
A mãe vai cantando
o filho embalando
canções mais suaves
lembrando essas aves
dos reinos de Deus!

A rede é também
caixão de defunto:
o morto dormindo
um sono gostoso
embalado na rede.
O morto, coitado,
não teve dinheiro,
não comprou o caixão,
e assim vai levado
embalado na rede
até que e jogado
no fundo do chão!

Lua-nova e uma rede
de prata, fulgindo
no céu tão profundo!
Deus descansa na lua
que linda, flutua,
vendo as dores dos homens
sofrendo, no mundo!

[3] "Hammock" in Portuguese: *Rede de dormir*, a net for sleeping. *Rede* is also used for a "net" as in a broadcasting network. Visual puns are easy to imagine—though not always so easy to film. To get the shot of the enormous ten-story high Embratel microwave antenna, we had to wait for the tide to go out, then dug post holes in the beach, then found the posts to set up a hammock in the foreground, so that we could shoot a close up of a guy in a hammock, then open out and tilt up to reveal the looming broadcast antenna. A thousand birds flew into view and circled the tower. This is one shot that definitely is more meaningful in Portuguese than English.

[4] The answer is "the hammock," but if you needed to look this up, go take a nap in a hammock and then read the essay over again.

REMEMBERING MAX MARTINS

Max and I were inevitable collaborators from the first night I met him in Belém do Pará at the mouth of the Amazon in 1985. I was there to teach a two week course in "American Culture," such as it was. Or what I could make of it in two weeks. My notion of a real place to start was, and still is, to screen lyrical documentaries made by Les Blank in 16mm film about Texas blues musicians. The 46 minute *Well Spent Life*, featuring Mance Lipscomb, remains a landmark of camerawork and insight into the American heart. Then images from the murals of Thomas Hart Benton would show the industrious strength of the United States alongside its residual weaknesses of poverty and prejudice. Finally I would rely on that Declaration of Independence, *Leaves of Grass*, Walt Whitman's 1855 book of poems, that not only broke the chains of literary servitude to Britain but transcended the bonds of imperialistic rime left over from the French invasion of Anglish in 1066.

Upon arrival at the airport in Belém, I lurched through the aisles of the tiny bookstore and grabbed up a bi-lingual copy of Whitman that sat alongside comic books and a newspaper that mourned the untimely death of Tancredo Neves, the president-elect of Brazil. That night about forty people showed up: students, journalists, artists, one psychiatrist, and a few poets. It was the most intellectually alive and diverse class I had ever confronted. I was introduced to Diógenes Leal, the guy who would run the slide projector for me. For the first meeting I planned on sticking to Benton. The carousel tray was already loaded with organized images of steaming locomotives and bumping dancers to illustrate the dynamic nature of the United States. I was ready, other than not being able to say much more than "Hello, I'm fine are you fine thanks." An interpreter had been provided, but Marcelo was as incompetent as he was enthusiastic, so I was counting on the images to carry the evening. Then a flustered Diógenes grimaced and said, "Não funciona." As balky slide projectors had betrayed me in front of the public more than once, I understood the situation. I went after the machine with my Chinese army knife and soon enough concluded. "Yes, it does not function." I was stumped, stymied, and literally speechless. The only remedy now was to: IMPROVISE.

The dual language Whitman was in my grief-case. I asked Marcelo to inquire of the expectant group whether someone would be willing to read the Portuguese. He explained the request and a general murmuring of "Max ....Max....Max..." soon resounded about the room and up came Max Martins, whom everyone in the room, but me, knew. Salt and pepper hair, owlish glasses, mobile mouth, and articulate hands, expressive even without his signature cigarette. (Max was one of the few people in modern history who really should have smoked. His style effortlessly out-Bogarted Bogart. And he made it beyond 82 years.)

For the next hour and a half we traded punches of poetry, Max first in a soft Portuguese that carried to the edge of the crowded room:

O broto mais acanhado prova que a morte
　　realmente não existe,
E se alguma vez ela existiu, levou a uma vida futura,
　　e não espera ao final Pará pegá-la de volta,
E pára no momento em que a vida apareceu.
Tudo segue Pará frente e Pará a fora, nada se perde,
E morrer é diferente do que qualquer pessoa supõe que
　　seja, e mais bem aventurado.

Then I read Walt's words deliberately, echoing in twangish American the measured phrases already heard in their native tongue.

　　The smallest sprout shows there is really no death,
　　And if ever there was it led forward life,
　　　　and does not wait at the end to arrest it,
　　And ceas'd the moment life appear'd.
　　All goes onward and outward, nothing collapses,
　　And to die is different than any one supposes, and luckier.

The duet concentrated the crowd into an intercultural trance as both languages sang together. The improvisation did not falter. After that class we went out for what was to be the first of a 1000 beers metabolized from the eighties across the nineties and into the oughts.

The next night the projector worked and Benton's vivid work precipitated an animated, somewhat fractured, discussion with occasional hissing at the interpreter: "STEAM! NOT STORM." After the class, the events that precipitated this poem happened:

REINCARNATION

and the street was narrow
     even for a shadow
nine lives, three poets
black
    cat under the wheels
    of the yellow cab
    scrowling thumps & squashing death
escaped

    "Eight!"

and the subterranean river speaks life
hidden
    by force
    of a fateful word
    turned against itself
springing through flat annihilation

our inheritance—
        death & life
        life & death
the three into one word: cat
black on white
            delivering us

REENCARNAÇÃO

e a rua era estreita para a sombra
sete vidas, tres poetas
negro
      o gato sob as rodas
      do carro amarelo,
         o grunhido
   da atropelada & esmagada morte
escapado

       Seis!

e um rio subterraneo diz da vida,
reclusa
      a pulso
      numa palavra azarada
      voltada contra si
saltando através da perda, aniquilando-a

herdando-a para nos—
    morte e vida
    vida e morte
os tres numa palavra: gato
preto no branco
         libertando-nos

Now it is a week and five meetings later when three generations of poets—Age de Carvalho (20), myself (40), and Max (60)—sit in the <u>3X4</u>, a friendly little bar on Flatiron Square in Belém. Our task is to forge a poem out of that incredible event which had actually happened to us the week before. This is how we wrote the poem: It was like a game of pool in which each player took a turn at a line, leaving the next fellow with a follow up shot that was sometimes easy, sometimes difficult. The pen passed from hand to hand three times round the table, until the poem finished itself. In a timeless hour three minds linked in series had produced a poem of one mind in two languages.

We each wrote in our own idiom, with Age translating brilliantly and sometimes breathlessly back and forth between American and Brazilian as we improvised. There are some small differences of detail. For example, I preferred the specific quality of "cab" to *carro* (car) in the line "under the wheels of the yellow cab / *sob as rodas do carro amarelo.*" This kind of freedom is justified already in that there cannot be an "original version" in a poem that is made simultaneously in two languages. Each version exists independently.

Some poems need keys to open them up. At the same time a poem, by its very nature, is playful and tricky and can never be revealed in its entirety. If it could, it would not be a poem. One key to "Reincarnation" is the incident that set it off. The week before we three had been headed towards the 3X4 after the raucous Benton class—which would have pleased the pugnacious Benton. As we walked along the dark street, the talk was about William Blake, mysticism, and at the very moment reincarnation came up, a black cat sprang out of the dark, ran over my toes, and directly under the wheels of a yellow Volkswagen taxi. The cat screeched as it was being run over, then miraculously came out the other side, leaping alive into the darkness. "*Seis*!" said Age as I said "Eight!" Sometime later we explained to each other that cats have seven lives in Brazil, whereas their cousins in the United States are customarily entitled to nine. Perhaps the tough climate accounts for the difference

(The conscientious reader will now go back to read the poems again.)

By the time the two week class was over, I could order a beer in Portuguese and ask directions to the bathroom, but beyond that I was still monolingual. Max spoke no English. But, when he talked Brazilian poetry, world politics, or impossible women, I COULD UNDERSTAND ALMOST EVERYTHING HE SAID. It was uncanny and even weird. Other articulate people I met spoke a blur of sound; but when Max offered his Amazonian insights on Charlie Chaplin, I understood. He commented on the cosmic equilibrium of the vernal equinox and I knew what I was agreeing with. It would be years before I could understand others as I could understand Max from the beginning, which induced a belief that communication precedes language. There was a congruence of minds, an overlap of understanding that mystified me in the degree of its clarity.

A couple of years later I returned to Belém on a Fulbright Fellowship to teach English and American literature at the Federal University of Pará. Having burrowed all the way through *Portuguese for Morons* since my last visit, I now had the vocabulary of a rather dim three year old; but in addition to being able to order a beer and a sandwich effectively, I could inquire about a person's age and origin. I spent numerous evenings with Max sitting at his side in front of the row house in the São Braz neighborhood he had lived in since 1953. Across the broken concrete street was a view of other row houses, a mess (*bagunça*) of electric wires, and the hulk of a bus station beyond the scrawny park at the end of the street. We drank good Cerpinha beer. He smoked his brand of *Free* cigarettes and we somehow conversed about the intricacies of writing and living. His voice was soft and lyrical and questioning and humorous. One evening I made a fateful declaration: "Max, I am going to translate some of your books."

There. I had said it out loud. I was committed. Or I should have been committed. Max' poems, unlike the direct rhapsodies of Whitman, are obscure, dense, and did I say obscure?—even for native speakers. His style is allusive, dark, and moving. (See *Madrugada: The Ashes*.) Where did I get off thinking I could translate his work? I know now: Fools wander in where Angels fear to stroll. We spent several evenings discussing various poems. Sometimes when I would complain about a particularly difficult stretch, he would say, "Ah, that's not my problem, that is a problem for the reader." Well, the word *madrugada* was a translator's problem for starters, since there is no single word in English for that most beautiful of Portuguese words that covers from the other side of midnight till just before the first rays of dawn. And for those who are out at such a rare empty hour: *madrugadores.*

Nonetheless, two years, dozens of re-writes, and various consultants later (including Professora Cerpinha), I had managed to conjure and to cajole a batch of his poems into American English. It was a baptism of mire. I figured that a third of the poems made a fairly direct trip across the languages, another third required gymnastic acts of imagination to arrive at an equivalent experience, and the last third were certifiably DOA—Dead on Arrival. (See *Isto Por Aquilo-II*.) The respectable *Latin American Review* and the wild *Exquisite Corpse* verified their viability as poems and translations by publishing a batch from the first two categories.

Our conversations and adventures continued. He liked the Beats and pronounced "Jack Kerouac": *Jaques Kayroo-ACK* He submitted to the *I Ching* and wished he could have drunk red wine with Han Shan. Often I visited his simple wood cabin near the isolated beach at Marahu on the island of Mosqueiro where Diógenes and I would film much of the *Hammock Variations*. It turned out that the slide projectionist was a first class cinematographer, who could shoot Max at his desk in available light seated at the foot of the wily monochromatic zen-tiger framed and lurking on the wall. Max became "The Poet" of the *Hammock Variations* that intercut "The Poet" writing a poem with a weaver weaving a hammock. Max was as videogenic as a practiced character actor. He could represent a poet composing like he was born to it. Well, he was.

Eventually in 2007 he had a stroke and that slowed him down considerable, but he smoked his way out of it and answered the challenge I threw at him to write a poem about returning from the dead to writing again. I told him an incredible story about a bat to get him going. He not only wrote the poem, but illustrated it with impromptu line drawings of owls that eventually figured in. His notebooks were grand quarries of clippings, quotes, receipts, and pornographic images outlined in grease pencil, born out of the jungle of his interior. To trace the evolution of a poem, from the expressive tangle of his journals, to a rough draft, to the finished poem is to appreciate the labour of creating a tantalizing shape out of chaos. Max floated on an implacably disturbing ocean and managed to sing both sweetly and harshly—and always persistently, about hidden glories well disguised in their origins.

It seemed like every time I returned to Belém, basically every other year since 1985, I would find Max on his stoop with some young poet at his side engaged in a dialogue of sincere inquiry and of laughing irreverence. One of those times I realized that the young fellow at his side had been me and was still me. I was a seekerish forty when I met him and he was an already ancient sixty. For the next 22 years our dialogue spiraled through time. He died yesterday, two weeks before my arrival in Belém, but I expect to hear soft suggestions of his voice for the rest of my days.

So long, Maxi.

PS: This postscript provides another unlikely corollarical turn of the screw. I recounted the story of the cat with 6 or 8 lives (take your pick) to my friend Gustavo in Goiânia and that led to this: During the same March of 1985 he and three pals were in the old City of Goyaz wandering about. Gustavo spotted the Church of St. Barbara atop a long hill. "Let's go up there for the sunset." They hiked up the rough road. Skinny Fabão had a harmonica, Roberto a guitar, and Bacana was responsible for the percussion, mainly with his rhythmic hands. Gustavo must have been the conductor of this garage-band outside the garage.

They spent the rest of the afternoon and the entire sunset like good Brazilians, singing songs of Milton Nascimento, Chico Buarque, and Caetano. They sang and gawked betimes at the spreading sunset from the steps of the Church until the stars heard their songs.

On their return they meandered down the road they had walked up—singing in joyous disharmony:

> How many roads must a men walk down
> Before you can call him a man,
> The answer my friend is blowing in the weend
> The answer is blowing in the weend.

And then around a dusty curve there was a body stretched across the grass grown road. Dylan's song stopped blowing. They gathered around the body determining that he was not dead, just dead drunk. They puzzled over what to do. Clearly he was vulnerable, sleeping it off in the middle of the two-track road, so they each one grabbed a hand or foot and lugged him off the road to the edge of a pasture, where they left him immobile but *breathing*.

The group set off again for a corner bar in the old city. But they had not gone 100 yards when a yellow Volkswagen beetle came bouncing and honking down the road. Then to their collective horror, instead of sticking to the road, the bug / *fusca* took a short cut to elude the curve and vroop vroop (Portuguese for "thump thump") and ran over the drunk in the grass.

"Oh my God, we have killed the drunk!"

They ran back to where they had stowed the man on the shoulder of the road. Fearful to approach, they heard him groan, he moved, he propped himself up on his arms, bleary eyed. He got up. Groaning. He dusted himself off, inspecting the tire tracks on his bruised arms.

Sometimes God does protect fools and drunks. The unbelieveable part of this story is attested to by four witnesses whose versions correspond in all details including the songs sung. The nickname of the drunk guy who accompanied them down to the bar with a slight limp was: Gato.

SELECTIONS FROM THE NOTEBOOKS OF MAX MARTINS

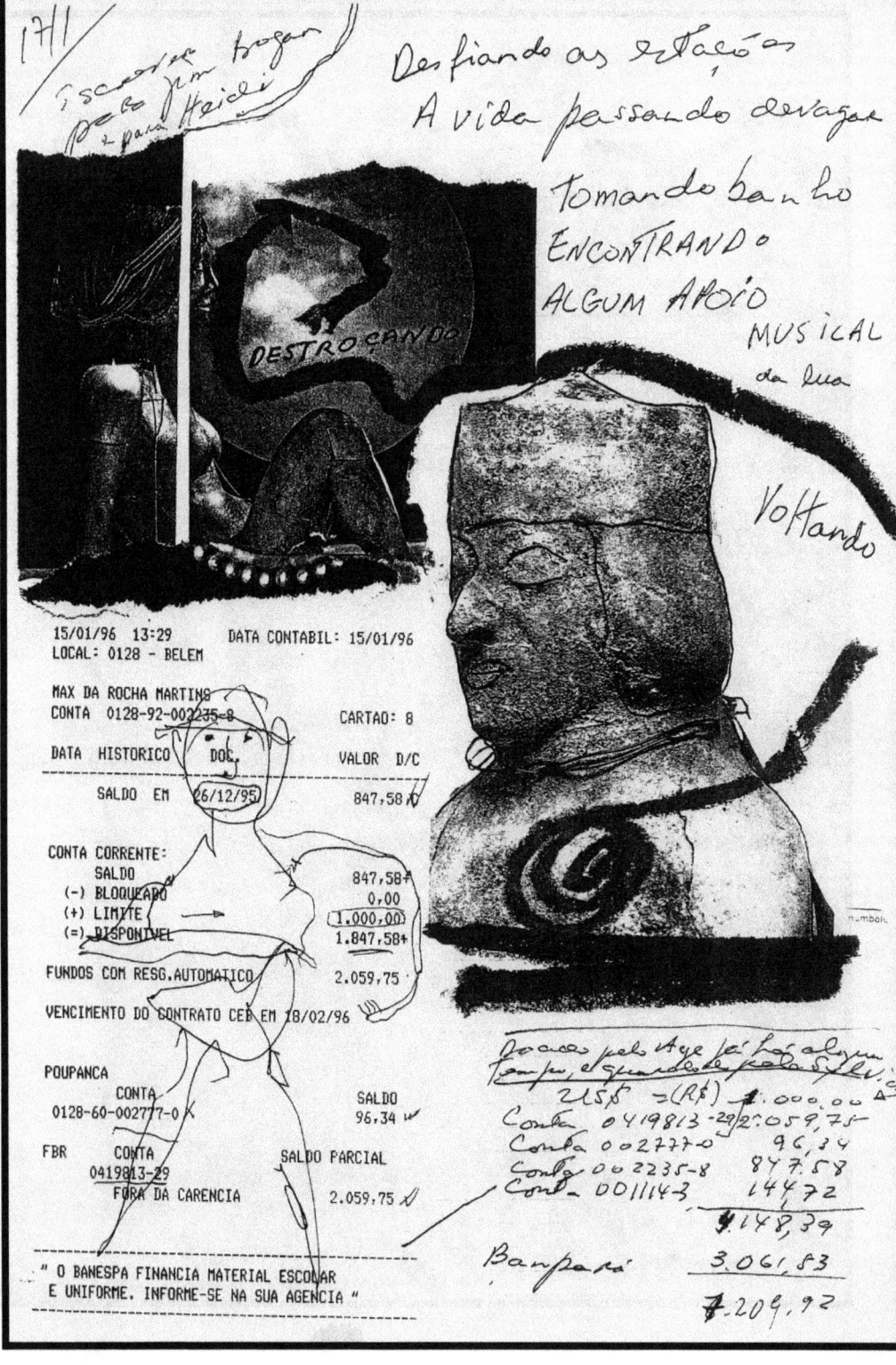

Confraternização
na Casa da Linguagem.

27 Dez

Quarante-cinq poèmes
de Yeats
L'Homme approximatif
de Tristan
TZARA
Stèles de
Victor Segalen
À la lumière
d'hiver de
Philippe Jaccottet

"Música incidental" Lou e Emília "Canta a ua jovem poeta"

MAX (His Mark)

A BATCH OF POEMS BY MAX MARTINS

Translated by James Bogan

Mar-ahu	**Mar-ahu**
Now it is not an island	Não é a ilha
Now it is not a beach	Não é a praia
It is the Sea we are making for only a name without	É o mar (de nos fazermos ão) é só um nome sem
a further shore	a outra margem

This for that (I)

It's impossible not to offer you:
The rancor of age in the burden of this poem
The roaring of a motor at the bottom of a bottle

        Or   this
(for that
vibrating
inside the breast)   heart in mouth
               behind glass   emptiness

               love blank and gnawing
        a rumbling motor

                         — rancor

Take:

ISTO POR AQUILO (II)   THIS FOR THAT (II)

    pro   pro
    por   pose
(sem dor)   (less pain)
   amor   love

as an example of:
from one tongue
to another
just won't go

To Shan-hui	**A Shan-hui**
This is not a poem	Isto não é um poema
yet	ainda
only hard work, a wall	é só trabalho duro, muro
of stone and nothing—	de pedra e nada—
a shovel	a pá
in my empty hands	nas minhas mãos vazias

*****

      This mare grazes
      the geography
      of my tomb
      to give me
      the milk of hell.
      In an ambush of heat
      her fire
      whips me,
      turns my liver
      into a stigma of mud.
      Now the fate
      of this rotted verb
      is to rot
      the sign of my meaning.
      She buried me
      and still I sing.
      Her kick was infinite.

The Cabin

You need to know your cabin is safe—
That roofbeams compass interior strength.
Listen: There is a swamp to cross.
It is not only deep, but ethereal.
Though there is a mat to sleep on,
Your cabin is not a place to stay,
Still it is a place to go.

*****

West. Not a drop of rain

West. No rain will come from that way
Nor are you going to find a plate on the table—your old modesty
Nor are you going to find Nadja, Cassie, Joanna, or Her
<u>Poesia</u>
drugged as She is
and prostituted—
stuck in your ancestral home

So hit the road
     (the wise man says so without words)
                       Lug your own dangers:

Don't expect your ancestors to meet you along the way
Someone will come from behind packing a knife
Your bird of sex is going to lose feathers in flight
Worse: In the forest your shack up in flames

Madrugada: The Ashes

These ashes greet you, *Madrugada*

As you mold the dark against the shadows
you mock the morning-song of this poem
you trap a fire burning blind in detours of blood

Again you raise a body on the sand,
Madrugada
cursed in a word, revived in a web
and rough shadow of black desire
bristling hair, the bitch of this page

Intertwined lines catch the fly of delight
already ruined, tenacious, fibrous—
an agony under leaves uncovers
the menstrual eye sadistic in destiny,
A dream grows, hardens—
a sexual rumble of echoes compounding

And the knock at the door
                      —hinges, pleasures in rust
the far off squeaking, the groaning from another world

At last,
Madrugada,
doubt traces a face
exposed in this mirror
held against the sun: Its spelling
reduced to ashes
calcinated

Madrugada: As Cinzas

Madrugada, as cinzas te saúdam

Do novo moldas contra a penumbra, maldas
o galo do poema, a tua armadilha, o fogo
arcendo cego nos desvaos do sangue

De novo ergues sobre a areia, madrugada, o corpo
armaldiçoado duma palavra, a teia rediviva
e a sombra crespa do desejo negro
eriçando o pêlo, o cão da página

Riscos se entrelaçam, fisgam a mosca do deleite
e já ruína
tenaz, fibrosa, agónica sob a folhagem, mostra
o olho menstrual e sádico do destino
Um sonho cresce e se entumece
no rumor sexual dos ecos se compondo

E batem à porta
              —os gonzos, os gozos da ferrugem
o rangido longínquo vagindo de outro mundo

De tudo,
madrugada,
a dúvida traca um rosto
exposto neste espelho
contra o sol: O soletrado
calcinado

The Cauldron

the sixty-year dream
of your life
(worm-eaten doors
open and close
close and open)

boils the fat and the claws of words
their shadowy liquor, your skin of remorse

                                        it boils over
the soup spills, the cauldron bursts

Buried is the jade pheasant
of your future
the tender bone
of your past

Now wood and fire combine again
and your number one enemy can't catch sight of you

Just go outside
sweep your shack
stick your tongue out at the sun—
such is your indolent hope

        the Korean tiger stalks the walls

It is correct to take another woman now
It is correct to mess up the bed
Read this ideogram
by the light of a dark

After Completion

Many years I walked with your counsels
With what you were
With what you are
                              I walked in your shoes

—water over fire

runic stone of words

Where will Saturday's bread come from?
Will the fox get his tail wet in this dirty river
And where is he going anyway?

The door beyond is closing now.
Will it be my turn when I get back?

Twilight Blue, Deleterious

The dwarf letter
malignant   from the missing star   Body
of wax and vice   Eye
of twilight blue of opium without consolation   Grain
of pale pink hate   Bitterbrake

                              (the trigger finger
                                the tough comma)

between eager eyelashes
silent   Island
between sleeping and waking   Letter
nothing-named   Orphan
unfinished
        unfinishing

And what damns me
                tames me
                              in this submissive fraud
                                            of solitude

An Ideogram for Blake

Bitter Id
and igneous tiger
                Tiger
within, a sub-
scripted line
             an arrow
traversing darkness

O

alone what remained
in the dream
of velvet-viced destiny
of that name
             leaks
from the mouth
of this poem
vessel of an acid nocturne

Ideograma Pará Blake

Amargo Id
e ígneo tigre
                Tigre
por dentro, sub
escrito risco
             seta
atravessando a treva

O

que restou só sonho
do veludo-vício do destino
desse nome
             vasa
dessa boca   do poema
                    vaso
do noturno ácido

Note: "What Is The Mystery of Poetry?" appeared in a 1987 Sunday edition of *O Liberal*, Belém's big newspaper. Several poets were queried. Paragraphs of profunduties were the stock answers. Only Max responded with a poem.

What Is The Mystery of Poetry?

The mystery of poetry is what's left:

    after the poem wins the big prize.
      after the Academy dusts off the poem.
        after the culture committee mops up with the poem.
          after the police-censors slam poet and poem in prison.
        after the pope blesses the poem.
          after professors extract meaning, metaphor, and paycheck from the poem.

The mystery of poetry is what's left:

    after the poem is entered in the Congressional Record.
    after a robot recites the poem.
      after they say, "Wow! What a poem!"
        after they say, "Oh! What a shitty poem!"
          after they don't pay for the rights to the poem—
      or even if they do.

The mystery of poetry is what's left:

    after the president quotes the poem in his Inaugural Address.
   after the thief steals the poem.
     after the Directory of Syndicated Poets takes charge.
       after the poet counts syllables on his fingers and toes.
      after the reporter asks,

"What is the mystery of poetry?"
    after the poet betrays his own poem by saying:
   "The poem is hungry for itself."

The mystery of poetry is what's left:

  after the oral poet surrenders his poem to the tape recorder.
  after Octavio Paz is devoured by the poem.
   after the psycho-critics isolate alienation from the poem.
   after the State fixes the value of the poem.
    after Borders puts the poem in the window.
    after consumers use the poem for toilet paper.
    after the reader encounters a poem face to face
     then erases it because he knows he doesn't know
     how to explain what he knew in the poem.

The mystery of poetry is what's left:

   after the poet turns himself off and signs
   his name in white at the bottom of a blank page:

A POEM AND SOME OF ITS STORY

POEMA INVISÍVEL

Tu ainda.
Ainda não estou aqui
Ainda não cheguei
            Tudo é irreal
Devagar tento juntar
        a cabeça ao corpo

Mas faz teu poema invisível
            impossível

— Morcego cego preso
    no olho do texto
            lá adiante.

Escreve-o. Escreve e me alimenta.

Poema Invisível	**This Poem Is Not Here**

Eu ainda.
Ainda não estou aqui.
Ainda não cheguei.
        Tudo é irreal

Devagar tento juntar
        a cabeça ao corpo

Mas faz teu poema invisível
        impossível

--Morcego cego preso
    no olho do texto
        da aranha.

Escreve-o.
Escreve e me alimenta.

It's still me,
though I am still not here,
though I have still not arrived.
        It's all unreal

How slow it goes
        connecting brain
            back to body

But to join your poem invisible
        impossible

--I am a stranded bat blinded
    in the eye of the text
        of the spider.

Write the poem.
Write and batten me.

TRANSLATOR'S NOTE: This is the first poem Max Martins wrote about eight months after suffering from a stroke that left him partially paralyzed, especially the left side of his face. He smoked his way into a recovery of three years before he died. I visited Max in Belém, during his recuperation and recounted the appended story of the bat. I cajoled him to use the image, but got only a sphinx' response for my cajolations; however, about a week after I had returned to the Ozarks, the handwritten *Poema Invisível* arrived in the mail, illuminated in the margins with a couple of strange entities.

Here's the story I told Max:

The white apartmented skyline of the city of Goiânia is visible from this ridge in central Brazil. There are a million and a half people on the horizon; but below us the Valley of the Rio Caldas is as empty of humans as Kaintuck Hollow, out of hunting season. It took about forty minutes to get here and is, as such, Gustavo's river of canoeing convenience. In lots of ways the Rio Caldas reminds me of an Ozark spring-flooded-brown river, rolling through farmland hedged with forest, in this case jungle. Swap the *Jatobas* for sycamores and factor out the palms and I would be back on the Big Piney, my own river of convenience. *Caldas* means "a hot spring" and the water today is rich as hot minestrone with runoff from the regular afternoon rains of this epoch.

Once on the sinuous stream, sharp maneuvers are needed to elude disasters and I am a bit confused by the litany of directions from my pal in the stern: "*Frente!*" "*Leme!*" "*Forte!*" as we crash through a veil of low hanging branches. Swept and drubbed. A familiar enough experience. But the reliance on the bowman for navigation is contrary to my lifelong experience and for a minute I wonder if it is because we are on the other side of the equator that this inversion is the norm. I find out later that a clever and strong paddler in the front is standard white water procedure, but we are on a river flooded fat over the rocks. The Ozark custom that the moron in the bow is there to gawk and the moron in the stern is there to steer should work here too. Gustavo and I try another protocol and he experiments with the demanding discipline of doing nothing in the bow as I take the stern and guide us, practicing principles formulated a full hemisphere north of here. There is an occasional spate of quick paddling; but our progress is swift and smooth, mainly, despite the occasional soft drubbing. Gustavo, a man of courage, sat low and centered when I pulled the old Ozark maneuver of "leaping the limb"-- clearing the felled tree across our course with only, uh, light lurch.

I feel quite at river-home and hope my continual comparisons to the Ozarks do not bore my companion; but really I am pleased with the similarities of current and flora, as in the chattering presence of *Martin Pescador*, the kingfisher's cousin. The bamboo is not all that exotic as there are groves of bamboo along the Eleven Point in southern Missouri.

But then:

    A neon blue butterfly big as a baseball cap flops by...

    A red monkey, the size of a five year old, leaps
       like a squirrel from one treetop to another...

    And that was not a turtle splashing out of sight,
       but an alligator....

        As in see you later...

           SOMEHOW
              I DON'T THINK
                   THIS IS THE OZARKS
                      ANYMORE.

And here is another one I NEVER saw in the Ozarks:

We are working our way up a *córrego*, a narrow, hairpinned, creeklet veiled in vines. The source of the clear water is some kind of spring and the sound of that invisible waterfall draws us turn by acute turn into this labyrinth that is happily without bugs.

Gustavo exclaims, "*Oi! Olha aqui! Meu Deus! Para!*" ("Hello! Looky here! Oh, my God! Stop!") Suspended eyeball high across the passage is a grey bat, his foot-long wings stretched out and hooked in a formidable spider web. We contemplate this weird apparition, hanging motionless but alive.... Gustavo even wonders if he is resting. I am looking around for the spider, when the trapped creature compacts into a fur ball and as quickly expands into a bat and flits off into the green jungle... Well I was dumbfounded with strange delight. In thirty years of Ozark meandering I never saw THAT before. "Nunca."

Only later does Gustavo admit that in his twenty years of extensive river ventures in Brazil, that HE has never seen the like. "*Nunca.*"

*****

In an attempt to understand "the meaning" of the bat-vision presented to us that day, I consulted the *Dictionary of Symbols,* which told me that in western civilization the bat is associated with disbelief, i.e. spiritual blindness, and in the eastern world, with longevity. I had figured the sighting was concrete enough and weird enough for a poet to do something with, so I dangled it in front of Max hoping to draw him out and he did all the drawing from there on. Perhaps Max has amalgamated the bat's diverse meanings...

******

A year and a day after my experience on the Rio Caldas I was canoeing on my river of convenience, the Big Piney, on a 70 degree day in winter with a 30 mph wind at my back—mainly. I saw the following: a three foot limb vertical out of the water with a cobra-like hood of wood at the top, that resolves to...to... a sun-dried turtle the size of my hand, clinging to the top of the stob. Is he dead? Certainly motionless. And he is apparently caught up in a spider web with strands that stretch to the next branch! He had climbed straight up to get the best of the sun in winter and is not eager to forsake his hard won perch. Yellow, green, and subdued red striations of color line his long neck. A dark eye glints as he does a back flip into the river, yellow-plate belly to the sun for a moment, then a dive for the deep where he disappears under a submerged boulder. An owl called from the woods. It is in the middle of the day. What IS going on here???

I must get Max working on the sequel.

******

Two years and two days after the bat encounter and a year and a day after the turtle encounter, I was back in Belém, back at Max's door, trying to shake another poem out of a poet who has rarely danced to the tune of another's muse, maybe once. I told him of the turtle, the owl, and the summer/winter.

"Go away," he said.

I went away.

The day before I was to return to the United States, we went out to lunch where I was the one who ate the grilled tucunaré and he ate steak.

"I don't think that is very patriotic of you, Max, to eat steak in sight of the mouth of the Amazon."

"I am a meat-man, man. By the way here is your poem:"

Um Quarteto de Improbabilidades

> Pia a coruja em pleno meio-dia
> Passo à passo a tartaruga sobe na árvore
> O que era inverno subito e verão
> Assim--tens a ver--o que--não pode ser.

"That's it. That's it! A veritable Gnomic quatrain! But it needs an owl. Can you draw an owl to guard the poem?"

"Easy." Whereupon he took the "sharpie" pen from my pocket and with his left hand made a couple of owls. "*Fácil*."

"But Max I never knew you were a lefty."

"Since my stroke for some reason I draw left and write right."

"Quite sinister."

***

Here is our poem:

A Quatrain of Improbabilities

When Turtle climbs a tree,
When Owl hoots at noon,
When Winter seems Summer,
Look to see what cannot be!

IMAGES ALONG THE AMAZON

THE ADVENTURES OF THE AMAZON QUEEN

The following three essays recount the some of the events both on and off camera involved in the making of *The Adventures of the Amazon Queen.* This half-hour, sixteen millimeter film, was produced over the course of 12 years through the persevering efforts of a crew on both sides of the equator. The film itself proof of the axiom that "Time is the ally of art, if the artist lives long enough." It is true that the producer/director was not in a hurry to finish the piece as it provided a compelling pretext for him to return to the Amazon.

Nonetheless, forward momentum, which sometimes appeared to be backwards, was maintained and the story of the brave craft's journey got told from the launch in a spring to the Ocean of the World itself. The adventure, however, was balanced on the fulcrum of the camera and what happened along the way was as marvelous as the sights that ended up on the screen.

In Search of the Rare,
If Not Non-Existent,
Blue Alligator of the Amazon

I am on the phone with Diógenes Leal, my cameraman-collaborator, who lives in Belém do Pará, at the mouth of the Amazon. Every one of my Performing Arts Department colleagues is probably aware of this call because I have a tendency to shout my Portuguese on these long, long distance calls:

"Tudo bem?" (How are you, fine?")

"Descobriu ainda um lugar a filmar jacarés?" (Did you find a place to film alligators yet?")

Once when calling a friend in Rio de Janeiro, she said, "I can't hear you over the line, but I am getting the faint end of a shout out the window."

One of the reasons I am going back to the Amazon is to get the last shots of the adventures of a hand-made model boat, the *Amazon Queen*, on 16mm film for a poetic documentary ten years, and counting, in the making. We still need two sequences:

1) The boat headed out to sea in the indisputable ocean. We already have the shots of the making of the boat from undifferentiated palm stalk carved and fastened into a scale model boat which covered thirty hours of labor on fifty minutes

of film, edit-reduced to five two-minute sequences. Then there are sequences in the can that take the boat from a spring to a little river to a swamp where it is attacked by an alligator to a river to a big river to the Amazon to the Bay that meets the ocean of the world fade to black... The last shot shows the Amazon Queen floating at the foot of the Statue of Liberty in the Port of New York. But there is no shot in the open sea, yet.

2) The editor does not like the cramped framing of the alligator chomping the prow of the Amazon Queen that we filmed three years ago at some danger to boat and Diógenes' cousin "Speedo" who earned his name fetching the busted up craft out of the alligator den. The editor wants more alligators.

And that has been the subject of my pre-class phone conversation with Diógenes. He has already filled out a long questionnaire for the authorities at the Municipal Gardens, a kilometer square of jungle surrounded by the 21st century, where we filmed the alligator attack previously but this time we are to have a committee of Park officials looking over our elbows. Such surveillance is not conducive to our improvisatory methods, so we will try our luck with this fellow who has an alligator ranch somewhere outside of Belém. He may even have a "*JACARÉ AZUL*," a blue alligator and they are big!"

Jacaré Azul. Wow.

I hung up and headed over to my French Revolution class, wound up on the exciting plausibility of filming huge blue alligators attacking the vulnerable *Amazon Queen*. Live. Maybe my students would like to know why I am going back to Brazil for the tenth time in twenty years? Why am I skipping the country for the expendable month of March and leaving them behind in the hands of my worthy colleague? What research befitting a University Professor am I engaged in?" Maybe the students in my French Revolution class might want to know and I certainly want to tell them:

"As I explained in my memo to the department chair: I have three main reasons to go to Brazil:

1) Film work. *The Adventures of the Amazon Queen* needs two more sequences to complete the film, and I need to work with local musicians to develop the sound track, and also I need to write the narration of the film.

2) To give a couple of lectures at universities.

3) Language study, especially with Professora Cerpinha, with whom I have spent many hours since my first visit to Brazil in 1985.

(Now Professora Cerpinha's resume was not included. Truth be told, I have studied at the best of language schools: the round table loaded with friends and all fueled by long infusions of the local brew: Cerpinha. I maintain that the combination of talk and indigenous fermented grains loosens the tongue effectively for articulating another language. In Italy, the reserved Professora Chianti is an inspiring tutor of Italian.)

My good chairman signed the memo and sent it upstairs.

"I just got off the phone with my collaborator," I tell the students, "and he assures me that we have a very good chance to film the rare blue alligator of the Amazon. So if anybody asks why your teacher has gone missing, just tell them that he has gone in search of the *JACARÉ AZUL*, the rare blue alligator of the Amazon."

The students were duly impressed by the mission, if not its connection to the French Revolution, which I have as yet to work out….

*****

I will spare the reader all the airport stories between the Ozarks and the Amazon. Eventually, I arrived in Belém and in short order was enrolled in my language course, currently meeting at the Bar Imaginario, where Professora Cerpinha ruled with cold smooth grace. Under her tutelage my Portuguese returned with force. I had not spoken but three hours of Portuguese in three years, the Ozarks being Brazilian poor. It was as though the language fermented during that time and roared to life when uncorked. Surrealistic paintings hovered on the walls. It was a dark dark evening. Worn out rain clouds hung between us and the growing moon. A toast to all friends and benefactors! And now, Diógenes, what about the blue alligator, jacaré azul?

"*Jacaré Azul*?" he returned.

"Yeah, the rare blue alligator '*jacare azul*' of the Amazon, with which you lured me out of the Ozarks to your city on the other side of the equator, by two degrees."

"*Jacaré Azul!*" He laughed. The people at the next table laughed too. "I did not say Blue Alligator, "*Jarcaré Azul.*' I said, "*Jacaré Açu.*"

"*Jacaré Açu*! You mean there is no *Jacaré Azul*?"

"I don't think anyone has ever seen one."

I was stunned but recalibrated my imagination and said, "Oh, *Jacaré Açu*, then. That sounds pretty amazing itself. The Rare Steel Alligator of the Amazon. Is it silver?"

He laughed again. So did the locals at the next table. "Not *Jacaré Açu, Jacaré Asso*."

"*Jacaré Açu*." I said it again. Originally this conversation was muffled via long distance international. You see how I could hear *Azul* for *Açu*, especially when seen on the film I am visualizing.

A fellow wearing a t-shirt that said "No Comets" stifled a guffaw in a glass of Antartica. (Another good professor.)

"No, not *Jacaré Açu*, steel alligator, but *Jacaré Asso* (ah'-soo)."

Putting the accent on the wrong syllable has its perils. For one, the difference between coconut ice cream and shit ice cream is the accent on *co´co* or *coco´*. I have made this mistake. At the time the waiter wrinkled his nose, deciphered my meaning, and served me a cone of coconut ice cream made with local coconuts. Excellent. Anyway:

"Oh, *Jacaré Asso*, Well what is "*Asso*?"

"Huge. It is the Tupi word for huge. *Asso*."

"Well, then we can film some Huge Alligators of the Amazon."

"Yes."

"I mean to keep looking for the *Jacaré Azul*, however…. I can see it. I have been seeing him for a month. Very blue."

"Sure, very blue."

*****

Before I get to the Alligator bit, I would like to detail how we did the shooting on the ocean. The plan was to go to Salinas, about two hours away on the ocean, but still in the wash of the Amazon. I had met a guy who had a "palace" on the beach. I was curious as to life in the palace. I mentioned to Diógenes that I thought I had digs in a palace arranged for Friday and Saturday. It was Thursday and we were on our way there. He was visibly uncomfortable about staying in a palace. Don't worry. It will be fun….

I don't think he was convinced.

About 20 kilometers down the road the sign indicated Salinas THIS way and Bragança THAT way. I remember an Elizabeth Bishop essay about Bragança, It has an old church. Diógenes lit up. Oh yes, and all kinds of old colonial buildings and blue Portuguese tiles.

"Now are you saying *Azul? Açu?* Or *Asso?*"

"*AZUL.*" He knew I was a sucker for *Azulejos*, the classic blue tile of the Portuguese.

"It's not much further. There is a beach outside of town, Juruteua, very very nice. And we can stay in a *chalet*."

"Well, maybe we could go there today and meet Marcos tomorrow in his palace. A *chalet* sounds good too. Big porch, eaves, on the ocean. Yeah."

"Maybe," mumbled Diógenes.

"Okay, let's take the road to Bragança."

So we swerved right and blew by the exit for Salinas. The two lane blacktop is a pretty good road especially after the potholes and washboard stretches on the main highway. Pasture, jungle, pasture out the window. Cows. Green hills like Ireland, but with palm trees."Wait a minute…. what was that place with smoke coming out and the gathered people. Let's check it out."

Diógenes u-turned us and went down a mud road a bit to the FARINHA FACTORY. He spoke with the photogenic head man, who did not want his picture taken, but for the rest of it and them, we should feel free. Diógenes balked at unloading the 16mm gear and I did not blame him but for the next half hour I took digital photos of the lovely people who worked in the open air artesinal factory to make *farinha*, a staple meal, which when cooked with butter and onion becomes the delicious and ubiquitous *farofa*, though it has not caught on in the Midwest of the USA. Third cousin to bulgur wheat/couscous, it is made from the manioc root and should not be confused with sawdust (*serragem*) which it looks like and when poorly prepared also has the texture of same. An older lady is washing the root over some kind of tub. The watery residue is called '*tucupi*" and is a prime stock for that Paráense treat *Pato no Tucupi*-- Duck in tupi broth with a few *jambu* leaves thrown in for trace elements... So I got a few shots of her lovely self at work and then I started looking around the tub, behind her bench, and she wondered what I was up to…. "So where's the duck? *Onde está o pato?*" She laughed. Her buddies laughed. The one year old in his mother's arms gave me a crooked look and cried. Ah, that one is a good judge of character. I got shots of the muscled fellow wielding the shovel over the wood heated iron pan of eight black feet across. It felt like time to hit the road, so we bought a one dollar big bag of *farinha* for seven and hit the road.

"So when do we get to Bragança?" I remember now that Elizabeth Bishop said it took a real long time to get there and the church wasn't much….Seems to be getting dark. "So how far is Bragança???"

"Oh, another half hour maybe…"

"*Hmmm*," which is Portuguese for "Hmmm."

An hour later we got to Bragança, I was used up, equatorially enervated. "Let's go directly to the beach. Sure, we can catch the church on our way out…."

After getting to the edge of the surprisingly large city, through the tropical night where it really gets dark fast and dark deep we got on the road that runs through the "*mangue*," swamp. "Is it far?"

"Well…."

It was far and featured plank bridges reminiscent of some scary bridges in the Ozarks before eventually we got to Juruteua and there did not appear to be anybody home. In the summer the place must be busy but in the middle of the rainy season not only was I the only gringo in the non-existent town, but Diógenes was the only city boy from Belém…. But there was a bare bulb burning at the FAZENDINHA. We traversed a rickety wooden platform and found the *barzinho*/office of the proprietor with the cute Mocinha at our service. We would like two chalets. Please. Sure. Ten bucks a day including three meals, but the beer would be extra. And the tide tonight will be enormous. The ocean was two blocks away invisible but loud in the total darkness and soon to shift in our direction. The *chalet* was not what I had envisioned, based on faded memories of Swiss Heidi prancing into a *chalet* adorned with scrolled eaves and window boxes. A more apt translation would be: *shack*. What we got was a slab-sided garage swaying on wooden stilts stuck in the sand. The doorstep busted in two when I put my weight on it. There was electric, which ran a light bulb and a socket, when two bare wires were twisted together. Connection was announced with an ozone inducing spark in a vibrant shade of *azul*. Home and a hammock at last.

Sometime deep in the *madrugada* I woke to the whoosh thump and shudder of an Atlantic wave breaking outside the door and under my floor. The door was left open in case the trust I felt in the flexible construction was not merited…. Whoosh thump shudder. I slept till the glare of the sun shone through the doorway.

It is time to film the boat on the high waves. Felipe is Mocinha's nephew, a hand-clever young fellow of fifteen. He catches on to the "plot" directly and is already attaching a monofilament line to the keel for an anchor to hold her in position for the turbulent waves of grey grey grey. Diógenes has already fixed the bad connection in the battery with his ever ready soldering iron. The camera is set up on the restaurant/dock space we have at out disposal. Felipe is going to set the boat in a spot that will surely be washed by breaking waves. The anchor is a baggie of sand. The wide angle lens will make the boat appear further out to sea and even smaller in the face of the breaking wave. Felipe walks through the surf and tosses the boat, and disappears from the viewfinder. Rolling film and the *Amazon Queen* pitches through some foam and then is totally overwhelmed by a rolling wave, water buried but then bobbing up right…. The next big wave washes her away completely and that is the last we see of her until five minutes later, when Felipe notices the little boat stranded against the pilings of FAZENDINHA, dismasted and about to be creamed. He jumped down to the sand, splashed over to the boat and snatched her up before the next wave that would have annihilated her. Then the mast surfaced from the brine. He grabbed that too…

    In short order Felipe was restringing the mast and Diógenes was filming the repairs, because we needed to return her to the sea and say one more "Bon voyage!"

    The next day was sunny and calm: the *Amazon Queen*, a tiny silhouette against the grey sea getting smaller… "Bon Voyage!"

    The End of this part, except for on the way back to Belém we got to stop in Bragança where there were indeed blue tiles and the 1798 slave-built church in honor of black St. Benedict and it felt a blessed holy place.

THE ALLIGATOR BIT

Upon returning to Belém, we called Jorge Artur about filming his enormous alligators. "It is a pity you did not call a week ago, because the Jacaré Asso has eaten. A few days ago. Thirty kilos of fish and chicken. Each. They won't be hungry for two weeks….But you are welcome to try."

"We'll try…."

A male and female *jacaré asso* and a few of their offspring lurk in the green lagoon. The little "huge" alligators are the first to have been bred in captivity. The male was in a word asso: Huge, as was his mate who was only about two thirds as huge. Tooth to tail he measured about fourteen feet and would surface to the sound of two hands clapping. The boat was rigged with a monofilament line to draw it across the murky water and a chicken leg strapped to the deck to interest the alligators. The *Amazon Queen* made smooth progress right towards the Huge Alligator, who submerged just when she came in range. And stayed submerged. Definitely not hungry and not threatened either. Well it made a nice shot of the boat playing chicken with a *jacaré asso*... Huge.

Let's try the other lagoon with the slightly enormous alligators. We moved the heavy Arriflex 16mm camera and wooden tripod. The setup looks like something off the set of Cecil B. DeMille. They do not make cameras this heavy, this bulky, this unwieldy anymore. Actually just setting up is an event and draws curious Alligators and even monkeys around the edges….

It is raining—what can you expect in a rainforest? Bill the Umbrella-Man protects the camera with an enormous café-umbrella. CINZANO—CINZANO—CINZANO. A menacing phalanx of medium sized alligators, seven-footers, pretends to be a backwash of logs. A twelve footer, an almost *asso* fellow, lounges on the bank smiling a toothy smile, if it is a smile. Ah, before we film the boat running the gauntlet of alligators surely to be destroyed, maybe we can get this fellow engaged in the action. Medium shot, and then we can see him leaving the bank and entering the water. Good.

"Okay, ready to roll."

"Ready,"

"Roll film and Action!"

"Action! YO, Alligator. IN THE WATER. NOW." (Not an eye blink.)

So I tried Portuguese: *"Ação! Oi, Jacaré. Na Água. AGORA."* *(Não um olho para.)*

"Cut."

This guy does not take direction well…. Let's try some bribery. Who has the chicken? Umbrellaman produces a meaty chicken leg. This will lure him off the bank. I tied the monofilament line tightly across the knee joint, if chickens have knees.

"Ready to roll?"

"Ready."

"Roll film, Action." I tossed the chicken leg end over end. (Ankle over thigh more accurately) and it splashed into the murky water about three feet in front of the alligator. Not an eyeblink.

"Cut."

I retrieved the chicken leg. The phalanx of twelve was lined up eyes at waterline, studying the situation. I figured I would just aim it for the big guy's nose on this take. I recall my early training at third base. I stopped more than I dropped and then fired over to first base with my strong, though somewhat erratic arm.

"And ready to roll."

"Ready."

"Roll film. Action." And I fired a Kentucky fried bullet towards the nose of the alligator and it sailed right over his head. It wrapped on a branch and dropped down swinging about two feet over his nose. Not an eye blink.

"Cut."

Now I remember one summer in my youth when I was banished to the outfield. I chased a ball to the fence and all I could hear were screams of "Home it! Home it! I grabbed the ball, whirled, and threw in a Willie Mays manner, and the throw had a direct line on home plate and the runner was almost there as the ball cut the plane of the plate, but, alas, it was about fifty feet above the catcher who watched it fly over the backstop, like a UFO—out of play, to say the least.

So the chicken leg is suspended over the head of the alligator. I wonder what would happen if I yank on the line…

"Ready to roll."

"Ready."

"Roll film. Action." I pulled sharply on the line and the chicken rose up and disappeared into the leafy branch which swung wildly startling the alligator who moved his three meter bulk from bank to water faster than the eye could take in but the camera recorded each 24th of a second.

"Cut. Good."

Now let's see what we can do with that phalanx of twelve, who had observed without audible comment the old chicken on a string routine.

"Ready to roll."

"Ready."

"Roll film." The *Amazon Queen* glides glides glides by the twelve rankled noses without incident.

"Cut." Even so, it is a curious shot.

"If you had only called me earlier, I assure you these fellows would swallow the boat in two chomps faster than you would see," said Jorge Artur. "Do you like snakes?"

"It depends on the snake. I certainly admire the Ozark Black Snake, six feet easy and ever so black and a menace to mice, not me."

"We'll see," he said and twenty minutes later here comes Breno, the snake guy, toting a six foot snake.

"Here," he says and offers me said snake.

"Is it venomous?"

"No."

"Will I bother him?"

"No."

I took the calm snake and wrapped him about. A very calm snake. With blue eyes! Actually eyelids, but very blue.

"This is Papa Pinto."

"Please to meet you. *Tudo Bom*?" The laid-back snake coiled comfortably around my neck and got his picture took. Then it was back to filmmaking.

"Maybe you would like to do a sequence with a boa constrictor—*Giboia*." Now here was an idea. All we needed was a boa constrictor. Ten minutes later Breno was back, with an *asso* boa constrictor held at a distance with his snake rake.

Well, the serpent was ten feet long, wide body construction, and cranky. Boas have teeth to hold their prey or your arm, so I kept fair distance.

We placed the boat on the margin of some brush.

(Photo by Diógenes Leal)

"Ready to roll."

"Ready."

"Roll film."

"Action! *Acao*! YO, snake, wrap yourself around the boat. Yo, snake…. *Oi giboia*…"

"Cut."

Boas make alligators seem easy to handle. Breno managed to wrap her around the boat.

"Roll film." The snake was not amused, but unrolled herself, gave us a dirty look as her head swung above the red painted hull of the *Amazon Queen*, and slithered backwards into the bush.

"Cut. Well done, snake." In the edit we can just reverse the shot and she will have come out of the woods, wrapped around the boat, and tipped it over….

Diógenes points out that it is almost dark and I ask if we have enough film to waste on his historical, "sure we can shoot in the dark" advice which has yielded some fine art shots in the past: white streaks on black

"No, it is really too dark."

It is time for another language lesson, which turns out eventually to be at a *churrascaria* on the way back into the city. Cerpinhas are on the table, excellent meats arrive every five minutes cut with sharp knives from leg sized cuts of lamb, beef, and pork. The waiter does not want to trade Lula for Bush. He is courteously amused at my continuing search for the jacaré azul. I had asked him, if he had ever seen one.

"No. Never heard of one."

Diógenes, then filled him in on the variations of azul, marking me a gringo with a dream. José Ribeiro, this waiter from Maranhão, was intrigued and offered to paint a jacaré asso blue, azul. I offered to buy the paint. He was to meet us on the corner tomorrow when we would return.

He was not on the corner waiting the next day.

And though I did see a flock of red red red red Guará birds flashing deep into the swamp, and though I saw toucans flying with their impossible beaks pointed north, and though I met a cabdriver named Angelo who had given me a ride ten years ago, I did not see the rare, if not-non existent blue alligator of the Amazon. I must go back.

Perils of Poetic Film Making

    Sometime around the age of twenty seven I realized I was a poet, based on the fact that I had written a couple of dozen poems in the previous two years—inspired by sudden love and the Ozark landscape, mostly. When I turned forty, I was still a poet, still writing about a dozen poems a year. I came back from Brazil with a poem about t-shirts backed up by a lot of slides of pretty locals sporting odd messages:

                Break the Dance
                Eternal Map of Love
                Yours for the Asking

The slides became a slide show, which I parleyed into a grant to make a movie and at that point I became a film maker based on the fact that I made a film, the Whitmaniac *T-Shirt Cantata*, which runs twelve minutes flat. Since then I have made a dozen "poetic documentaries," and some of them are outright "cine-poems." James Broughton of *The Bed* fame is probably the most complete cine-poet there has ever been. He clouted me a creative clout on the side of the head. So did Les Blank, whom I first met while he was editing *Burden of Dreams*, the best movie ever about what it takes to make a movie. I like to think that my image-driven films are "cine-poems," a term I was pleased to have invented, until I stumbled on a short reel of *cine-poemes* produced by Man Ray in 1923…

T-Shirt Cantata was the overture to my unlooked for career as a film maker. *Tom Benton's Missouri*, a half-hour film about the cinematic muralist's sensational painted walls in Jefferson City, required a long fast four years to complete. Then it was years to produce the *Hammock Variations*, which proved my dedication to the hammock as a way of life. The Missouri Research Board even awarded me a research grant to spend three months swinging in a hammock reading four thousand pages of Patrick O'Brian and struggling through *Rede de Dormir,* in Brazilian, the unparalleled opus on hammocks by scholar Câmara Cascudo. I knew I was on to something when I deciphered the "Canticle of the Hammock," a poem which totally recapitulated the "plot" of my film. This discovery confirmed the validity of my take on the hammock. The film follows the weaving of a hammock, intercut with sequences of the revered Amazon poet and pal Max Martins at work composing a poem about how:

> Everything happens in a hammock—
>   from before we are born,
>   along the arc of our life,
>   til they carry us to the boneyard
>   to rest up till Judgment Day,
>   it all happens in a hammock

But the incredible story of the poem-narration for *The Adventures of the Amazon Queen* really lays out the curious and involved process of poetic film making. Here follows how to write a film script in fifty-five years, two hours and one week, with a technique not currently taught at certified film schools. Remember: Time is the ally of Art if the Artist lives long enough.

The Adventures of the Amazon Queen had been in production for about eight years—or eleven—depending on whose memory you want to rely on. The director/producer/sub-editor/writer/grip—that's me—thought we started in 1996 with a filming trip upriver aboard the *João Pessoa Lopes* in four days to Santarém and back again to Belém in three; but Diógenes, the cameraman/producer/grip/body guard—claims we shot boat footage during the final days of production on the *Hammock Variations* in Vigia at the mouth of the Amazon in 1993…. That we ultimately used only a minute of the two hours we shot on the river trip and none from Vigia still leaves the question unanswered….

"When did you start on *The Adventures of the Amazon Queen*?" The inspiration for the film goes back to my childhood and the three-tiered white bookcase in the "front room" stuffed with a motley assortment of books thumbed and gummed dog-eared by my two older sisters. *Friendship Farm*, I remember, and *The Little Train that Could*, which also included a 78 rpm vinyl record in a sleeve inside the cardboard cover. Very cool by 1950 standards. But my favorite was *Paddle to the Sea*, published in 1941, by Holling Clancy Holling, who wrote the story of an Indian boy in Canada who carves a small canoe out of pinewood and turns it loose for a voyage into Lake Superior, and points east, over Niagara Falls and ultimately to the Atlantic Ocean. The greenish hard-back cover was scuffed and bent up, but inside, the vivid illustrations of "Paddle" stuck in ice, silhouetted against a full page forest fire, or floating in a beaver pond, fascinated me more than I knew. To this day I am not sure I have ever read all of the educational text, but I am confident that it is quite educational.

Sometime after I landed on the Ozark Plateau I thought about doing a film about a kid who would put a model Johnboat into Prewitt Spring then watch it float out of sight on the Big Piney, to the Gasconade, to the Missouri, to the Mississippi; and the same kid would eventually fetch it up again on the other side of the Eades Bridge under the St. Louis Arch. Ideas are cheap. Nothing ever came of it.

Maybe it was in 1996 that I needed a solid pretext to return to the Amazon so I could continue my language studies, which amounted to drinking beer with friends, my idea of a really effective "total immersion" language school. Thus was I was motivated to come up with another project which would require my presence in Brazil.

Diógenes had the industrial weight Arriflex 16mm camera with the shoulders to support it. Traditionally it was my responsibility to come up with a concept (a high toned word for a cheap idea) be it t-shirts or hammocks, plus enough film stock and cash to get production going. Boats. I love boats. Let's do boats: A boat on the Amazon, intercut with a craftsman constructing a *barquinho*, a model boat which he will send to the Sea. It took five bi-annual forays to Brazil to do all the filming and keep up my language studies. One dimension of the film as originally conceived was a day in the life of a working boat on the Amazon. In 1999 we shot some amazing stuff aboard the *João Pessoa Lopes*: like, running aground on a sandbar while trying to dodge a three hundred yard long raft of logs coming downstream at us; the crew unloading 1000 cases of beer in Almerim; and then there was the race with another steamer into the sunset. All but two minutes of that fabulous footage ended up on the cyberial cutting room floor, because it made our film just too complicated and too long. The working boat had to go.

By 2002 we had a lot of the film shot, but were missing several essential parts, including the alligator attack and a final ocean sequence. I would have to go back to Brazil AGAIN! Now I like my films image-driven, which is to say, I edit them visually first, as though it were a silent film, which is what I did. The "brute cut" of forty-five minutes was in hand for the twenty-eight minute film, but not a word of narration was penciled in. If the *Amazon Queen* was ever going to make it out to the ocean from the interior, the narration had to get written. I write, but prefer to write from inner compulsion, not from external demands like deadlines. This attitude is not "professional" and has been derided as "intolerably romantic" by some reputable poets and accountants. Edison's phrase that inventions are "1% inspiration and 99% perspiration" seems to be more pertinent in these MFA/MBA days than Wordsworth's emotion recollected in tranquility or sources like Blake's, "who are in Eternity." Since I have a day job, I can afford my anachronistic aesthetics. Nonetheless, I was getting a bit anxious about when the narration was going to show up.... But it did and here is how:

Sometime in 2003 I had been on a visit to my journalist son Jesse in San Antônio and had made it to the airport in regulation time before the return flight to St. Louis. The line for the security check was interminable and slow. I waited patiently, knowing that my Swiss Army knife was not going to be confiscated this time, because the authorities had stopped me and it on the outbound leg at Lambert Field. Did I want to go back to the American Airlines counter and check it through? Did I want them to melt it down? I said, "I will be back," and retraced my steps, knife in hand, about twenty yards, where there was a plastic potted palm. I buried the knife in the fake gravel and hoped I was not caught on a surveillance camera. Maybe it would be there when I got back.... So in San Antônio I was not worried about my Swiss Army knife when my shoeless turn came to go through the x-ray, but they stopped me anyway.

"Sir, we need to go through your briefcase." Sure, I said wondering what stray item caught their attention this time. I had already off-loaded scissors, toe nail clippers, and a copy of the Koran.

"What's this?"

" Oh, that is my flask of spirits that I carry for protection against snake bites and frost bite. I never had any trouble with it before."

"You cannot take it on the airplane."

"But I have carried it on numerous flights without problem."

"You have a problem now."

"You mean you want me to pour out the last of my Locke's 8 year old Irish whiskey?"

"We don't care what you do with it, but it ain't going on the plane. NEXT."

I was sent to the end of the line and the time for my flight was getting uncomfortably close. The last of the Lockes was not to be wasted, even if I had to be… So I obscured myself behind an empty flight desk and drank three hefty shots: one, two, three. Zim. Zam. Zoom. I got back in line, and hummed Coltrane's version of *My Favorite Things*, in a consciously subdued manner. When I met up with the security guy again, I turned my opened flask upside down politely and was moved along…. I grabbed a long cup of coffee and got into the plane and sat down just as they shut the door. Now what.

My leather legal pad folder was balanced on the tray by the time we were fifty feet off the ground and I block-printed:

THE ADVENTURES OF THE AMAZON QUEEN

Then I scrawled:

The Artisan:

> Bon Voyage
> my Amazon Queen,
> built to last,
> built to lose
> the moment
> I set you
> upon the water

and I kept writing without pausing, like the boat swept along in the river's overwhelming current…..

Somewhere over Lubbock I switched from the Artisian Manoel to the Voice of the Amazon Queen:

> I am a dream queen.
> I command forces
>   of buoyancy,
>   of draft,
>   of balance,
>   of forward momentum…

The words poured out in a torrent from the breached reservoir in my soul where this theme had been fermenting for fifty-five years. At cruising altitude of 36,000 feet, the Amazon Queen was saying:

> The engine of this voyage is fueled by desire.

I write recklessly, not caring about punctuation or spelig, so long as the words roll out of the cheap ball point pen lifted from an airport hotel:

> My wild faith
> and obstreperous imagination
> beholds you emerging
> from jungle streams
> onto the big river…

The stewardess asks me if I want a drink. "Nope."

"A snack?"

Again with the "Nope."

The words boil up like the earth-pressurized flow of an Ozark spring—Blue Spring: The Amazon Queen says:

> As the sun sets,
> I am poised
> to venture
> beyond
> the embrace
> of land…

I write and write and write without a pause for two hours. Finally Manoel says:

> I set you
> upon the water
> that will,
> Lord willing,

> carry you
> to the Sea.
> Bon Voyage!

It was an end and we were just now starting our descent into St. Louis. I would check tomorrow to see if the narration was really there. The whole story had arrived in poetic blood pulses of whiskey-fired concentration. Out the window an obscure band of the dark Mississippi borders the lights of Missouri and Illinois. My head was clear for unblurred gawking, so I must have metabolized all of the Locke's in the clean burn of inspiration. There had been no time for thought. The plane hit the ground like a crate of oranges dropped from a pickup truck.

In the corridor alongside the security warp, I remembered my Swiss Army knife, designedly dropped inside that potted palm. I dug into the gravel and the red knife came to hand and no guards descended upon me....

The day after my return from San Antônio, I checked the manuscript to see what I had. It was indeed a poem. Later on I spent some twisted time deciphering what I had transcribed from the ether, since my handwriting is execrable and has been since second grade, as all my elementary school teachers reported and those who receive postcards from Tierra del Fuego these days will also confirm. But the first draft was now typed into the computer which told me there were 777 lines. The narration was in the boat and the boat was in the narration.

*****

A year later in 2004 I stood on the stage of the Bi-National Center in Belém after a screening of *Hammock Variations* and a bi-lingual reading of *Trance Arrows*, accompanied by Iuri Guedelia on flute and Walkyria Magno e Silva on Portuguese. I do not like making promises, but distracted by the euphoria of performance, I said the words. "I promise I will be back in March of 2006 with the Amazon Queen in hand, *se Deus quiser*. (Lord willing.)" Now I had done it. Later that week we got the Ocean scene shot and some contextual alligators but I hadn't untangled the narration and it still looked like it had just gotten out of the jungle.

A week after my public promise on the stage in Belém, I was sequestered in a farmhouse on the banks of the Rio Caldas in the boondocks of Goiás in central Brazil. I had taught writing courses across the Seventies and, as refugees from those forced marches of words would recall, the great secret of good writing is re-writing followed by more re-writing as long as the writer can possibly tolerate. An occasional nip of whiskey might help, too. I spent five days re-writing and re-writing and re-writing what had appeared in those two hours on the plane the year before. It was all there, except for a line or twenty that appeared as needed as I re-wrote and re-wrote. I wanted the narration to have an archaic epic feel, like some equatorially displaced Anglo-Saxon sailor's lament. That emerged too. The narration was written and re-written.

In the next year the film went from brute cut to rough cut to a rather fine cut, all without reference to the words, so *The Adventures of the Amazon Queen* was totally "image driven," like a silent film and the words would find their proportionate places later.

Later is now September of 2005—three months before the announced premiere date in Rolla, but the film still needed its male and female narrators: Manoel the artisan and the Amazon Queen herself. The first fine cut of the film had scratch tracks in place. I read Manoel's part and the good Jo Ella Todd, an opera singer, delivered an enthusiastic reading for the Amazon Queen. Unfortunately both of us were disqualified by nature of our Midwestern accents and ideally these voices would be in American but lilted with a charming Brazilian accent. The scratch tracks did provide guidance on expression and timing but we could not have Manoel sounding like he just escaped to the Amazon from the South side of Chicago or the Amazon Queen herself an operatic diva from Arkansas.

I telephone-tested a half dozen potential voices, but none hit the balance of clarity and accent that I thought I was looking for. "I'll know it when I hear it." Usually it was not enough American and too much Brazil. One girl from Rio read the part perfectly, too perfectly as she sounded just like Jo Ella—just another beautiful American voice. Time was running out and nervously I prayed to St. Anthony—a casting director's last resort--to find me some voices.

I was headed to San Antônio once again, this time to visit with Jesse, before he took off on a scary but necessary three month assignment to Iraq for his newspaper. My flight was on September 8, but I decided to go into St. Louis the night before to attend a Brazilian Independence Day party at the Bar-Celona where Moacyr Marchini's Band, *Samba Bom*, was playing. I had collaborated with Moacyr and his partner Kathy Corley on *Hammock Variations*. But now I need VOICES. Charmingly accented voices.

When I arrived the street party was swaying to a steady samba rhythm emanating from the band that was stationed on a patio. Moacyr was playing guitar and the occasional whistle. I joined Kathy at a round table on the sidewalk. We embraced and I proposed a toast to Dom Pedro I, the clever emperor who gained independence for Brazil without having to resort to a revolutionary war. It was in the era when Napoleon was menacing all of Europe and had fatally invaded the Iberian Peninsula, taking Spain in name, if not on the ground, and he had designs on Portugal too, England's old ally on the continent. Do not forget that much of the English gold that suborned the world was actually refined Brazilian ore from Minas Gerais, escorted to the Bank of England by the English Navy. Anyway, there was Dom João, King of Portugal in Lisbon, not getting a good night's rest because of the incursions of Napoleon's army from Spain. Wellington could not guarantee the royal family's security, so along came a radical plan: The King of Portugal with his family would decamp to Rio de Janeiro, the capital of his huge colony to elude the depredations of the power-crazed Corsican. So, the King passed his time on Guanabara Bay waiting for the Emperor to blunder himself into his own double exile.

The family, including the heir apparent Pedro, left behind the gold gilt of Lisbon, the ancient dull stones of the city, the drizzly winter and the steaming summer, and took up residence in a palace in Rio de Janeiro ringed with rich hammocks, served by suave *mulatas* surrounded by exotic but accessible jungles. Lush green mountains framed everything against the warm blue bay: Rio de Janeiro before *favelas*, before air pollution, before street crime. It made the Garden of Eden look like a cheap resort.

Eventually Spain and Wellington bled France into weakness and Napoleon's disastrously managed foray to Russia broke his hold on Europe. The royal family was free to go back to the old palace, but what do you know, the son basically said: "Tell you what, fellas, I will just stay here and keep Brazil for myself. You can have Portugal. Anyway, I would rather be a king here than a prince there. The emeralds will be mine and we can share the language. The old man can have the stash of gold monstrances piled up in the Lusitanian monasteries…" (That is a free translation of a heretofore unpublished and unknown memorandum from Dom Pedro to the aristocrat tutors of his younger and ultimately rebellious brother Miguel.) The memo is dated September 7, 1822 and for this reason we are now dancing in the streets of Clayton, Missouri, on September 7, 2005, a Brazilian community in exile shouting: "Independence or Death!"

When the group returns to a round table on the sidewalk there are four others besides Kathy. Moacyr is playing "Demasiado." Just like they say that everyone really wants to be Irish, so everyone, including the Irish wants to be Brazilian. Next to Kathy is a guy from Uzbekistan and then a girl from Izmir that used to be Smyrna, and two Brazilian women. Ah. Kathy backs up my claim that I am filmmaker looking for a beautiful Brazilian voice, not a beautiful Brazilian. I hand them each a script, give them a minute to look it over, and ask them in turn to read a few lines. Elena reads in a clear but halting fashion, somewhat in the manner I read Portuguese, then the other one says the lines and they are not merely spoken but it is a kind of muted singing, soft and articulate. This is the Amazon Queen herself.

Her name is Andrea Azoubel Loveman and she is as dark-eyed pretty as her voice is melodious. An architect, originally from Recife, she works on the other side of the river in Illinois. She is at this party because Michael, her husband, plays keyboards in the band. "Would you be interested in the part?"

"Well I never did anything like this before.... But yes, I would like to try." And here comes the good part: "My younger brother speaks English better than I do..." She calls him off the street where he is dancing a restrained samba with a girl from Romania. His name is Guillermo—that's William to us—and he is as blond as his sister is brunette. "Gilly [think Willy] this man wants you to read something." He reads some of Manoel's lines and he is Manoel. And here is maybe the best part. The band is taking a break. Moacyr introduces me to Michael Loveman, husband to Andrea, a wiry fellow of luminous blue eyes and a concentrated manner. I explain the lightening casting that has just taken place during the last two songs. "That's great," he says, "and by the way we have a recording studio in our apartment." I am stunned with this blow of good fortune, especially as I have already been wincing over how I would have to rent a studio in St. Louis and make several trips to the city to oversee the recording sessions and pay the stacked up bills... I was afraid to ask, but it was the big question: "What kind of microphones do you have?" And the answer was the best I could have hoped for: "The best." Not only could he record in his home, he could also do the final voice editing. In twenty minutes everything came into place. I testified on the spot to the powers of St. Anthony.

When the band went back to work, we toasted Dom Pedro I. We toasted St. Anthony. I danced in the street celebrating all the freedom that comes of being in the right place at the appointed time, with a renewed confidence that *The Adventures of the Amazon Queen*, this Sisyphean dream of a lifetime, was actually going to get done in due time.

And eventually it did.

SCREENPLAY

THE ADVENTURES OF THE AMAZON QUEEN
[Content of sequences is noted inside the single brackets.]

Amazon Facts

The true headwaters of the Amazon in the Peruvian Andes, 4185, or so, miles upriver of the Atlantic, was not verified until 2001.

The Amazon has more than a 1000 tributaries, ten of which are longer than the Mississippi.

By volume, the Amazon is the greatest River on Earth, with a flow larger than the Mississippi, Nile, and Yangtze combined.

I) VOICE OF MANOEL=VM
[Manoel places the *Amazon Queen* in the creek and waves good bye.]

> Bon Voyage,
> My Amazon Queen!
> Built to last,
> built to lose,
> the moment
> I set you upon
> the water
> that will,
> Lord willing,
> carry you
> to the Sea.

II)
[Superimposition of AQ over map of the Amazon]

THE ADVENTURES OF THE AMAZON QUEEN

Produced and Directed
by
James Bogan and Diógenes Leal

III.) VM [Arrival of Miriti]

>My nephews are fetching
>the miriti palm branches that will
>become through my hands
>a boat bound for the sea.
>My name is Manoel
>and the name of my boat is the
>*Amazon Queen*
>but she does not exist yet
>except for a shape in my mind
>and a pulse in my hands.
>
>I sit
>home
>in one spot
>hour
>upon hour
>upon hour
>upon hour
>concentrated in creation.

I sit at home
in this one spot
to send you out
to the ocean
of the world.
I sit still
dedicating
my finger-skill
that you may endure,
with engineered strength,
the terrible challenges
of days and nights,
of currents and backwash,
of moonlit roots and sun-washed shoals.
What will become of my boat…
depends on mindful hands now.

IV.) VOICE OF THE AMAZON QUEEN=VA
   [Creeklet, rain, mud]

Manoel's hands release me
to a dripping spring branch
of clear water.
His hands inform all my being
and now I am seeking the sea
for which I was born…
The unnoticed initiation
of my journey
begins in a spring pool
connects to a creeklet,
a small boy could leap,
 yet it is one source
of the great river's power.

I am a dream queen.
I command forces
of buoyancy,
of draft,
of balance,
of forward momentum.
Released to the current of an Amazon tendril,
I have joined the ways of the water.
One telling push and I am on my own.
One sinuous turn and I am gone.

A debt I have to my maker
but enough it is
to keep my way
downriver—
to see just what is
around that next bend…
All rivers begin small
and draw to themselves
countless increments of volume,
some infinitesimal
and none insignificant.

A savvy guide
in the shape of a boy
directs me towards the sea…
This brave boy,
who was born
on this river's edge,
 already
handles his paddle
with the skill of a lifetime.

The rain comes and goes,
comes and goes,
filling the banks to full.

The word is *caboclo*
for this man
of river and forest,
who paddles his way
in a landscape blurred
by slanting rain.

And who has not been stuck in the mud?
And who has not been retrieved
through the slogging help of a friend?
Who has not… probably is not any longer.

V.) VM [Making boat]

    Amazon Queen!
    I offer you
    of the long power
    of the indifferent river.
    You will survive
    because I have instilled in you
    the water-wisdom of my uncle
    who taught me
    and those who taught him.

    Generation upon generation
    have thus instructed me
    in the way of waves
    and the pull of the wind
    and more:
    The keel of creation is love.

    Dream bark!
    You float

across
my day-dreams
to Belém,
appear
in my nightmares
attacked in a hostile swamp.
You reappear
rescued
by a stranger
who understands
your journey,
who gives you back
to the water--
reborn

VI. VAQ [Iemanjá, Turtles, Alligators]

Iemanjá's pond is enchanted.
There is no place this peaceful.
This is the dream
of the Amazon Queen,
moored
at the feet
of Iemanjá,
invoking protection—
protected.

The engine of this voyage is fueled by desire.
The desire of my maker propels me forward
The angle of his will lifts my bow
 through parting waters.
The bow wave chants the hope of his dream.

Cruising, cruising, cruising—
I am the elfin queen of the Amazon,
animated and propelled
by interior forces.
I exult in fanciful
motion forward
and cannot pass up
the chance to shake up
Eschelons of lazy turtles.

Who knows
what is around the next bend?
Nobody knows.
But I am determined
to find out.

In silent backwash
I have come to rest,
in rounded repose
ensconced among
regal lily pads....
It is not much of a mystery
that I echo Manoel

VII.) [Alligator attack]

VIII.) VM
[Manoel constructing hull and afterdeck]

>Though the *Amazon Queen* is small,
>she will be strong.
>Though the miriti palm is soft,
>she will be tough.
>Her ribs joined to the backbone of her keel
>will absorb the blows of wave and wind.
>My cunning will lift her prow.
>My patience will hold her hull together.
>The flat of my sharp knife
>is hammer enough.
>Amazon Queen,
>I build you
>to ride waves
>where I will never go.
>
>You are fashioned
>to follow the current
>that sweeps through the village
>around the bend
>to the creek,
>through swamps,
>to the big river.
>
>Maybe you will arrive
>in the great city of Belém do Pará,
>only to be pushed back
>on the flood of the moon-pulled tide
>then sent twice-fast forward,

as the ebb combines with the current
to turn you towards the sea.
My fond wish is
to cast you free
upon the water
that will take you
way from me,
focusing here
of my mind's
crystal eye
to behold you
cruising down the river,
a replica of a working man's boat
with a ready hold,
and still a queen
in bearing, elegance, and balance.
Yet fretful fears
nag
my visions,
for you are headed
towards the mightiest
of all earthly rivers.
Disaster seems inevitable.
What is left but prayer?

IX.) VAQ [Boatyard]

Fonseca found me
washed up
and takes me to his backyard
boatyard
for needed repairs—
a nose job.

By my busted bowspirit,
I wish that reptile had choked!
I guess I got off lucky.
Though I cannot say,
"I escaped the jaws of an alligator,"
I did escape
FROM the jaws of the alligator.
With reason Manoel built me strong
and Fonseca rebuilds me
stronger than ever,
but no more for me
the perilous precincts
of proprietory alligators.

[AQ accompanies a fishing boat]

This guy looks like my big brother.
We share the family likeness
of cunning design
so apt for these waters,
so time-tried and space-traveled
that small or large,
we go, we go, we go.
And like two horses
prancing on land,
we vie for the lead
which I take—
Or maybe it is given
with an older brother's indulgence.

[Headstand]

Sometimes,
raretimes,
I am not the most peculiar sight
on this river headed to the sea....

X.) VM
[Manoel constructs the rail, bowspririt, rigging]

> I sit still hour
> upon hour,
> as you take the full
> shape of ship.
> *Amazon Queen*!
> To be launched
> in a creeklet
> yet bound for the sea,
> bound by my dream
> to follow
> the falling water
> that leans to the deep.
>
> You are a child sent forth.
> Your heart is the interior
> and from within
> you venture out
> around the bend
> aimed
> where I have never been,
> and never will be.
> You go on your own,
> but you go as emissary.
> You carry the form
> of my dream
> of my love
> of my skill.
> You are suffused with care,
> which guarantees you nothing—
> but promises much.

XI) AQ—[Sunrise-noon-sunset]

> A day can seam a month to the future….
> At noon God does not rest….
> A month can seam a day in the past….

XII) [Port of Belém]

> Belém… Belém do Pará!
> Great city at the mouth of the whole Amazon.
> I will cruise the Ver-O-Peso market
> and "see for myself the weight"
> freighted in this old port .
> This is my promenade of a city whose
> stones have witnessed much since 1616.
>
> Great freighters,
> ships of the sea,
> unload and re-load.
> ready to return to
> the Port of Piraeus
> Cadiz
> Dakar
> Said
> Bombay
> Shanghai
> Adelaide
> Yokohama
> San Francisco
> Panama
> Port of New York
> Your homes are my destiny.

Passenger boats head back
to where I came from—
now
long ago.

Belém is where the Amazon meets the sea.
Here is the last stop for those traveling out
of the interior
and first safe haven for those crossing the
sea from Africa.

A wicked wake
swamped me
before I knew it
in a treacherous channel
where bigger boats
than I
have been overwhelmed.
The daring kindness
of an unknown friend
returns me
to an equilibrium
I am warned to maintain.

XIII.) VM [Manoel paints boat]

    I sit still
    to fill
    your frame
    with the intelligence
    of my ancestors
    beyond memory
    in the quiet house

on my dusty street.
I know you will please others
with your inborn elegance.
Luck-pluck will somehow see you through.
My wild faith and obstreperous imagination
beholds you
emerging from jungle streams,
onto the big river
onto the Amazon
over the waves of the sea
the Atlantic sea,
the Ocean of the World.

XIV.) [Boa Constrictor]

XV.) [Dag with the *Amazon Queen* on bicycle]

I do not even remember where Dag found me—
Washed up, hung up, stuck in a root wad—
I do not remember.
Dag is a pilgrim
as I am a pilgrim.

His odyssey around Brazil,
intersected my voyage
one day.
He tells me of his journey
in memory of a lost brother's dream.
He talks to me—
everyone who has picked me up
has talked to me.
This day is Palm Sunday
which is why Dag has rigged

my mast with a pennant of palm,
tree of my material soul.
He rededicates my voyage
in the niche
of the stone-old church of Our Lady….

    His prayer is for one
    who has endured much—
    to endure more.
    In this
    he prays
    for himself, too.

Dag holds my shape and knows the hands of my maker.
Too bad he and Manoel can't drink a beer together
to toast my departure into the Ocean of the World…

    Ancient Vigia,
    First town of the Amazon.
    where river, bay, and sea converge.
    Here I exercise my powers
    in protected peace,
    cleaving the waves in sharp thrusts forward,
    cruising the town in a farewell lap
    for I am at the edge of the sea.

    As the sun sets,
    I am poised to venture
    beyond the embrace of land.
    Fishermen return home.
    I left home long ago
    and will not return.
    In the pacific reflection

of this sundown
I gather my power quietly,
ready tomorrow for the open sea….

XVI.) [Pan from Princess Diana poster to Manoel rigging sail]
I sit still
And still I sit
painting the soft fibers
of the light wood.
I bent the planks
that formed the prow
that will cleave
the waters of the river
to gain the sea.
I will ballast your hold
to roll with
overwhelming waves
and return to keel even
again and again and again.

I rig you with a triangular sail
to augment your heart-driven power.
All true sailors revere this ancient pattern.
I sit still in the doorway.
The room is swept clean.
I have concentrated the power
of my carpenter's arm
into the transom's
perpendicular strength.

[AQ on waves]
Beware, oh, beware,
my Amazon Queen,

        the treacherous following sea
        that will try to breach your back.
        All you can do is
        accept the push
        and balance the response
        with decisive instinct
        But no man's love will prevail
        and no man's skill will outwit forever
        the punishments of the unbridled sea.

XVII.) [Boat fix]

XVIII.) VM [Manoel paints name and "Put me in the water…"]

        I can see you,
        my Amazon Queen,
        beyond belief
        safely harbored
        in Bahia's Bay of All Saints,
        in Buenos Aires,
        venturing
        around the Horn—
        Why not?
        ((SUBTITLED: Please put me in the water,
        that I might gain the sea))
        And beyond: Easter Island
        Tasmania and Calcutta
        washed to sea again by the Ganges
        tossed around the Cape of Storms
        and by the estuary of the Black Congo
        under the shadow of Gibraltar
        with zigzag course more random
        than brave Ulysses'…

XIX.) [Boat in creek]

> Bon Voyage,
> my Amazon Queen!
> Built to last,
> built to lose,
> the moment
> I set you upon
> the water
> that will,
> Lord willing,
> carry you
> to the Sea.
> Bon Voyage!

XX.) Credits

Manoel da Silva—The Boat Builder
Dag—The Bike-Pilgrim
Fonseca Junior— Boat Fixer #1
Felipe Gonçalves de Sousa—Boat Fixer #2

   Produced and Directed
       by
  James Bogan and Diógenes Leal

    Cinematography
      by
    Diógenes Leal

   Narration Composed
      by
    James Bogan

Voice of Manoel—Guillerme Azoubel
Voice of the *Amazon Queen*—Andrea Azoubel Loveman

Translation to Portuguese by Walkyria Magno e Silva

Executive Producer—Frank Fillo

Editors
Online—Michael Hicks
Offline—Ryan Wylie
Additional Editing—Tom Shipley
Additional Audio—Mitchell T. Hill
Assistant Editors—Frances Stafford
      Ross Payton

Music Composed by Iuri Guedelha

Musicians
Iuri Guedelha—Flute & Saxophone
Mauro Ricardo—Guitar
Davi Amorim—Guitar
Jacinto Kahwage—Percussion & Keyboards
Kid Galivan—Additional Percussion

Boat Handlers
Captain Fonseca
Captain Pinga
Mary Bird
Anna B. Monders
Bello O. Garoto
Weures "Speedo" Carvalho

Sound Design—Ryan Wylie
Sound Engineers—Jacincto Kahwage
                      Michael Loveman
                      Claudia Schauer

Angels—Roger and Beverley Moeller
Unit Production Manager—Shelly Plank
Associate Producer—Ryan Wylie
Assistant to the Producer—Lori Voss
Umbrella-Man—Bill Yeazel
Stunt Double for the *Amazon Queen*—*Rainha do Amazonas*
Fact Checkers—Scott Peterson and Selden Trimble
On-site Inspectors—Brendan and Lt. Lisa Bogan
Technicalities—Brian Matt
Title Development—Max Tohline

The plot of *The Adventures of the Amazon Queen* was inspired by Holling Clancy Holling's *Paddle to the Sea*, one of the great books of Northern Literature.

Post Production was completed at the Cooperative Video Group at the University of Missouri.

Special Thanks To:

The Moura Family of Belém:
    Maria Jose, Moura, Marcia, Monica and Nana
The Family of Manoel de Jesus Pereira da Silva
The Family of João Batista de Sousa
The Family of Marcos Borges
The Family Fazendinha
The Captain and Crew of the *João Pessoa Lopes-II*
Marcos and Teresa Ximenes
Kathy Corley and Moacyr Marchini
Emmanuel and Francimeire da Silva
Max and Lais Martins
Steve and Eliana Jeanetta
Jo Ella Todd
Lynn Fair
Bridget and Clark Keitel
Jesse Bogan
Stuart Haynes
Courtney Haynes
Fred Goss and Ellen Pearce
The Family of Caetano Soraggi
Alan Kardek Guimarães
The Sisters Hicks: Alexandra, Jessica, and Madeline
Iracema Amarante and Jorge A. Leal
Marcia Dias

Claudia Silveira
John Francis
Michael Arnegger
Wayne Cogell
Richard Miller
Susan Kellems
Karen McGee
Harry Gate
Annie De Souza Martins
Will Vizuete
Barbara Bloch
William Stedman
Danilo and Simone Fernandes
Santo Antônio
Paula Lutz
Russell Buhite
John Fulton
Les Blank
Werner Herzog
Ross Haselhorst
James Broughton
Craig Miller
Joaquim José da Silva Xavier
Steve and Aurea Alexander
Domingos Maciel de Carvalho
Jorge Artur
Senhor Barzinho da Cariparinha Bar
Professora Cerpinha
Nonato Loureiro
João Gomes Neto
All Refugees of Art 85: Study of Film (1975-2007)
The Keitel Arms—Webster Groves
Missouri-Pará Partners of the Americas

The Partners of the Americas
Federal University of Pará
Casa de Estudos Germânicos
Bosque Rodrigues Alves
ABDeC-Pa
KMNR
KUMR
MHL Productions
Academic Support Center
Crocodillo Safari
Pousada Fazendinha
Cinema Mocorongo
Bar Balofa
Midas Amazon Studio
Delara Travel Consultants
MSM/UMR Alumni Association
UMR Department Arts, Language, and Philosophy
Distinguished Teaching Professors' Fund
Video Communications Center University of Missouri-Rolla
University of Missouri-Rolla

XXI.) The most recent sighting of the *Amazon Queen* by Elmer Davies of Maries County, Missouri, while on vacation in the great city of....

[*Amazon Queen* floating in New York harbor under the Statue of Liberty]

                Copyright...2007
                Dark River Films

TWO SCREENINGS

I. The Good One

Tatanyá literally means "burning moon" in Tupi and figuratively is their word for "star." *Tatanyá* is the name of Eddyvaldo's thirty foot boat that took us to Abaetetuba, about eight hours upriver of Belém and the place where we had filmed Manoel constructing the Amazon Queen ten years ago. We arrived at sunset and moored alongside another wooden boat at the municipal pier, whose fat timbers bent under a massive load of brown bricks. Locals had advised us to arrive before dark in order to be safe from river bandits, *piratas*, and so we were sitting on creaky stools at Rosangela's cafe, eating some kind of fried fish well before the sunset reds faded to blacknight.

For centuries Abaetetuba has been a center for sculptors of carved boats, birds, and snakes, all made from the *miriti* palm branch. Before time immemorial Tupi tribes did the same, but not with metal blades. Lately the brightly painted objects have included miniature computers, i-pods, and cassette players. It is a living tradition, but boats, birds and snakes still dominate the subject matter. Our objective was to find Manoel and to arrange for a screening of *The Adventures of the Amazon Queen* where it was shot. We circulated some ancient photos of Manoel among some of the artisans we met the first evening. Nobody knew him. I feared him dead, or at least gone and lost in the big city.

On the usually busy Saturday morning, boatloads of people come in from the hinterlands in canoes, motorboats, and skiffs to gather supplies of rice, beans, clothesline, and on down the long list. In quest of a cup of coffee, I was threading my way along a main street crammed with bicycles.

I passed up a dose of salted alligator and even the prized *pirarucu* on sale in the tarped over stalls, when by beautiful chance I spotted Manoel pedaling down the crowded street. The moment I saw him, he saw me. I divested myself of backpack and he dismounted from his bike. We embraced. I think I jumped up and down in the middle of the street. Except for his hair being the least bit longer, he looked the same. He had heard there were people looking for him and by some kind of karmic inevitability—you have to call it something strong—I had bumped into him on the street. He was fine, but no longer made *barquinhos*. He had a wife and two little kids. His family was fine. He had long ago given up on seeing whatever became of the Amazon Queen he built and put in a creek.

Right now Manoel is on his way to work at the *frango* factory, where he carves chicken, not miriti palm. We arrange to meet up on Sunday afternoon at the dock, where the *Tatanyá* is now safely moored. A restaurant is situated at the end of a dock that reached out into the river and is equipped with a sizeable television with a really good sound system, mainly for watching soccer. The proprietor said we could use their excellent big screen to show the film. The occasional fishing boat--*popopo*, diesels by and the audience will be well supplied with the Guaraná or beer of their choice. GOOD CONDITIONS.

At 4:30 Brazilian time, Manoel arrived with about 15 members of his immediate family, all of them dressed to the nines…. *Domingueiros*—in their Sunday best. Manoel introduced his sisters, who had been little girls the last time I saw them and were now looking after little kids themselves. I remembered in particular the green eyed one. He then presented his wife and displayed his two children, one a baby.

The now complete audience of 40 or so includes a group of wood carvers, a journalist that helped us out ten years ago, other locals. In a quick introduction of *The Adventures of the Amazon Queen* I make extended reference to the tradition of boat and *barquinho* making in Abaetetuba and the heroic job Manoel had done in constructing the Amazon Queen under direction of a stranger who had him repeating many of the actions over and over again.

The film began and from frame one to frame last I could feel the intense concentrations and recognitions from the audience. They saw themselves as kids, as artists, as *ribeirinhos*—river folk—featured in this quotidian but exotic film that lyricized their lives. At the conclusion of the film when Manoel says his: "Bon Voyage, my *Amazon Queen*!" and sets the built-boat free, I saw the tears in his eyes. We had made a true film. During the credits when the postcards appeared from London, Port Said, Paris, and beyond, the audience's laughter accompanied the *Amazon Queen* on her cosmic quest.

During the ten or twelve years the film was in production there had only been one strenuous disagreement between Diógenes and myself. After he read the narration, he was dubious. "These words are rhythmic and poetic, but I just don't think your average *caboclo* thinks like this way." Well, I ain't about to re-write it and at the very least I bet while your average river guy wouldn't use a word like "obstreperous," he would at least recognize an "obstreperous" feeling. And furthermore, one of the ancient tasks for a poet is to articulate what defies articulation.

After the credits and copyright ran their course, Manoel came up to the front of the assembly and I took my chances and asked him a dangerous question, "Manoel, when we filmed you for the thirty hours it took you to make the boat, you said very little. Actually you said nothing, but persisted in a focused concentration the whole time. I have to ask you about the narration you yourself speak during the film, a narration I wrote for you. Did you indeed think those thoughts?

"*Eu pensei*. I thought them."

Diógenes brought the alligator-busted/ocean-pulverized stunt double *Amazon Queen* forward. "I know you have quit *barquinho*-building for now, but I wonder if you would undertake the renovation of this travel-weary boat?" His dark eyes popped as he took the battered boat he built in his hands and turned it over and around, inspecting the damage. "Yes, I will repair the boat, but I will leave the tooth-marks of the alligator."

II. The Wicked One

The previous evening our friend Pinheiro had arranged a screening at the College of Saint Anthony, a school run by an Italian order of brothers in an ancient complex of buildings with a thick columned cloister at its center. Tall palms stood at attention outside the auditorium packed with enthusiastic students and the projector worked.

Tonight the show goes on at UNAMA, The University of the Amazon, a modern facility on the edge of the city. The eight-story building is an oasis of organization and education amidst tire-repair shops, steel depositories, and God knows what else behind graffitied walls. Pinheiro has done it again: 200 students and professors in a modern auditorium, a working microphone, and a DVD projector ready to go.

So I am blasting away with an introduction that I have had some practice in, explaining in my now serviceable Portuguese that we are going to watch three poetic documentaries on the subjects of t-shirts, boats, and hammocks, each one featuring an artist at work, and set here in the Amazon. I ask, "Who has a cell phone?" Half the room raise their hands. "Who has not disconnected?" Nobody raises a hand, but half of the half is busy punching buttons. I explain that filmmakers really hate to have the rhythm of their films interrupted by a trance-breaking beepbeepbeepbeep. Spectators do not like it much either. There are general murmurs of agreement, as the lights dim…

Dancing my way in front of the screen, I am lit up by the opening credits of the *T-Shirt Cantata*. A few rude whistles follow me to my seat screen right. I am ready to sit back and enjoy the audience who, measured by the laughs and smiles at the sight of: "Belém," "Cowboy," and "Bad Boy" are enjoying the film. They roar in happy memory when the legendary giant kangaroo atop a pickup truck smash-cuts into view, accompanied by a shift in the music from polite mandolin to blaring saxophone. It is a filmmaker's dream to watch his film in the presence of an enthusiastic audience. Then a beautiful freeze frame of a lovely girl in a long "James Dean" t-shirt holds the screen. Whistles of appreciation. Except I never noticed a freeze frame of this lovely girl. Maybe I should have lingered longer on her fetching face but I had not grease pen marked the work print 20 years ago to indicate to the lab to freeze a frame for five seconds at $20 a second. The film stutters a bit and moves along. It is just a glitch—just a glitch and nothing more.

As the credits roll by, my red laser pointer emphasizes "Professora Cerpinha." Around here everyone gets the reference. After a pause in black, it is on to *The Adventures of the Amazon Queen*, except the narration track is garbled: "Brn vooge, mm Azn Kin," and then non-existent, leaving only an undulating music track. The images are okay, but the narration is lost lost lost. The audience becomes righteously restless, and I squirm in my seat at a total loss. Diógenes is already conferring with Paulo the Projectionist back in the well appointed booth and I think about calling the whole thing off, but then an event from my own days as film series impresario in the Ozarks pops into my head.

Perhaps it was in 1976 and we were being visited by a relatively famous British director, who stopped in Rolla to pick up $400 cash on his way between Washington University and the University of Kansas. He had made a quick introduction of his film to a sizeable audience of 200 assembled in the St. Pat's Ballroom. Tom Elliott, the student tech fired up the 16mm Bell and Howl warhorse projector and there we were following the early career of Edvard Munch in a great shot of a schooner delivering the young artist to Oslo, at which point the director himself stood in front of the image becoming himself a phantasm of film. He shouted at Tom to turn the projector off. Now. The sound was not quite right. Tom re-threaded the 16mm-gauge celluloid tightly around the sound drum so that the rollers floated with tension and turned it back on.... The words were quite intelligible, though somewhat muffled—not a bad average in those optical track days and par for the 16mm course. "TURN IT OFF," the director shouted. With little experience of stereotypical artists, I was too dumbfounded to tackle him and drag him off to drink a beer or something. The screening was canceled and the audience invited to return the next night for another try.

As I sat squirming in my hard plastic chair in the auditorium at UNAMA, I remembered the negative example of the temperamental artist, but this machine is REALLY screwing up my beautiful film. By this time, it has been re-booted, re-chapterized, and re-dvdeed on a backup machine. The problems remain as Manoel places the *Amazon Queen* in the creek and waves a bon voyage, except he is not talking and the music is coming and going and I am on my feet, across the front of the room, waving a bon voyage in silhouette as I pass in front of the image and grab the microphone and commence to make up a new narration on the spot in Portuguese—not my native tongue and without the aid of Professora Cerpinha... Necessity is the mother of interpretation. At the beginning I can easily remember the repetitious narration:

I sit home
in one spot
hour
upon hour
upon hour
concentrated in creation.

Me sento
num canto quieto
hora
após hora
após hora
concentrado na criação.

When the *Amazon Queen* appears, I start talking about how, "My trip begins in a spring and I am born for the sea...." It ain't ideal, but it is working, and I hold my own for a few minutes against a relentless stream of images in need of clarification, and here is the sequence where the boat is attacked by the alligator. The audience gasps and shrieks appropriately and I can feel that this improvised narration is actually working. I let myself feel a burst of confidence, just as some silicon circuit hiccups to repeat the alligator sequence again.... And I realize the salvage operation to hold the narration together is doomed and the only unreasonable option left, short of bailing out, is to create a new film as it shifts before my eyes.

"Looks like it is time to feed the alligator again! Look out, *Amazon Queen*!" Wham. "O wicked greedy alligator." I must say it seems a lucky turn to get this scene twice, but then it appears a third time. Diógenes and the projectionist are scratching their collective technological head in the booth. I am way beyond worry as someone in the audience shouts: "*Cuidado, Rainha!*" WHAM.

The next scene actually appears as it should with Manoel building the boat. I interject how the film was edited visually first, how it really works like an image-driven silent film, and how even without the narration the story should still work—at least that is THE THEORY. "Note the interior construction of the boat, ribbed just like a real boat." Manoel taps the wooden sliver nails tap tap tap with the flat of his knife just as the music/sound effects track decides to amplify itself by a factor of five and the tap tap tap becomes BANG BANG BANG, the flat of his knife becoming a sledgehammer on an iron spike—BANG, BANG, BANG. Now I claim we are in the early days of sound, recapping scenes from *City Lights* and *Singin' in the Rain*, when a cell phone goes off.

A girl about three rows back is dimly lit by the cell-screen and she is fumbling with her phone, as I leap into the seats to seize the offending apparatus, which she shoves into her bag. We arm-wrestle a bit—her soft hair smells of lavender--and I come up with the phone, like a fish grabbed out of barrel. She says, "It's my mother." I am in front of the screen painted by a scene of the Amazon Queen blithely coursing down the muddy river:

"Hello!"

"Yes, your daughter is fine."

"No, I am from Chicago."

"Listen, we are having some challenges here during class and I must return to the lecture..."

"Well, I will be free after 10..."

"*Até Jacaré*!" ("See you later, Alligator!")

The audience applauds and yells its satisfaction at this gorilla technique for dealing with cell phone interruptions. I return the phone to the girl with a wink. (I suppose I should be candid here and fess up to the fact that the line was dead at the other end, but I have executed variations on this routine in classes early every semester since cell phones turned up and it is an amazingly effective vaccination against such outbreaks.)

Back to the film just in time to ask the audience to do its own commentary to the shot that shows a city in the distance across a bay.

"Where are we?" "Belém!" they call out in unison.

I get to resume the narration as the *Amazon Queen* cruises at the water line along the steel hulls of ocean-going freighters and I can remember most of its dreamt itinerary:

> Piraeus—Cadiz—Dakar—Bombay—Shanghai
> Adelaide—San Francisco—Panama—New York
> Your homes are my destiny.

Then the random powers of the projector emits gross crunching sounds on a dark screen followed by the revelation of a boa constrictor unwinding from the boat and the snake's ever-so-slow patterned retreat into the jungle. That sequence needs no commentary, nor does it have any.

Now the boat is being tossed by breaking waves, now it is being repaired and released to the ocean, and now we are back with Manoel in the interior by the creek and he sets the *Amazon Queen* free and I provide the "*Boa Viagem*," and the credits roll long enough to show postcards from London, Port Said, Shanghai, and it seizes up on Sydney Harbor with a disproportionate *Amazon Queen* in the foreground. Santo Antônio, the ubiquitous Professora Cerpinha, and Harry Gate get extra screen time before I shout: "CUT! LIGHTS!" We made it to the end and the beginning. The audience applauds and shouts "*Viva Rainha do Amazonas*!" They have not seen the film we made, but they have witnessed and participated in a creation which I now declare to be DADADACTICISM, an improvisation including aleatory elements of fractured film history, egregious editing technique, and even theatre-etiquette. The spirits of Marcel Duchamp, Man Ray, and Vertov may have been in attendance. James Broughton was there.

To conclude the evening's mayhem, I am ready to give away a miniature *Amazon Queen* to the first one who can answer the question, "Who has been the worst president in the history of the United States?" Since the answer comes in another unanimous chorus of "Bushie," I award the boat to the poor girl whose cell phone went off and then I sincerely thank the good Pinheiro, hassled impresario of the evening, for this unique (I hope) and astounding opportunity. Then we head off for a seminar in the Portuguese language led by Professora Cerpinha.

THE STREETS OF BELÉM

I cannot walk down a block in Belém without some dang adventure or uncalled for insight befalling me. Sometimes I get to throw a net of words around the experience and end up with a poem…

Four Meetings

I.

The Race

Walking along Aveninda Presidente Getúlio Vargas
headed for the river-bay
I had been already warned.
"Belém is more dangerous than ever"—
That is a superlative sorry to hear.
"Forget your camera.
Use all your attention.
Stay alert.
Don't walk.
Take a cab."

After being interned in the basement of the Hill Town Hotel
poaching their internet I am ready to walk
the ten blocks to the port in the late afternoon.
The busy commercial street is Low Down Saturday
empty
after Carnival,
after Ash Wednesday.
in the relief of a well-earned Lent.

So I stride down the blocks
disguised in my plain clothes and trashed tennies,
alert for pickpockets
though the lack of crushing crowds
does not favor that particular felony.

So far so good.
I even manage a slow 360 degree turnaround
to check if I am being trailed
and walk on until accosted at knee level
by a recently licensed two year old
who wobbles in front of me.
I catch him and pat his butt three times
before setting him on his own trail
towards his laughing mother.
I walk past where the good coffee place
used to be.
I walk past the shuttered photography shop
where I used to take my film to be developed into slides.
And in the very spot by the post office
where my old friend Ruti
had her post card stand is sitting
a shady character all by himself.
I steam on by only to hear at the back of my ear:
"*Americanos sempre tem pressa…*"
That is, Americans are always in a hurry.
It's relatively true. True for me often enough.

I turn on a dime and sit down next to him.
"*Não Sempre*," I say. "Not Always."
An impressive scar runs across his right eye
and into his cheek.

At my unexpected maneuver
his face opens up, does not sharpen
which would really be a bad sign.

"Yes, I am in a hurry,
but my race is not for business.
I am headed for the sunset
and nobody can outrun the setting sun."
In a few minutes we both agreed
that the world was "*Tudo azul.*"

We shook hands
and I walked off at a much diminished speed
in a subdued dance towards the river.

He shouted after me: "*Meglior!*"
That's better.

In front of the Bank of Brasil
there was a clot of ten drunks
standing around a bucket.
Some were really drunk, some more ambulatory,
which is a bad mix for a wandering scholar like myself
but as I moseyed by unhurriable
their attention was riveted on a bucket.
One of their number studied his cheap Rolex watch.
Serious bets were riding on just when the rat would drown.

I arrived at the dock in good time
to catch the glorious gold of sun and sunset
A hammock moon appeared in the west with Venus attendant.

The race was mine.

II.

The Exemplar

I did not attempt the walk home miles across the dark city.
THAT would have been stupid.
Instead I took the taxi at the head of the line
with a *licença* as I sat in the front with the cabbie.
"How long have you been driving a cab?"

"Forty-seven years—without a ticket."

"My lead foot disqualified me from that competition."
Early and often.
He is soft voiced and alert.
Born in Belém, he drove the city
as it grew from 200,000 to two million.
He may have had to elude a billion potholes,
but not once did he have to deal with ice on the road
like I did in Chicago.
Safely delivered to the portal of Almeida Bancrevea
I give him a tip from "one cabbie to another!"
He accepts it with a smile that confers a benediction in turn
as I absorb the luck and attention of a contented cabbie
who never got a ticket in forty-seven years.

III.

The Pickup

I found her
on the street
near the main square
dressed as for
a photograph
neat,
with a heart of gold
dangling from one ear

Maybe she was twenty
maybe sixteen, no less
I picked her up
maybe a little Indian blood
a dark-eyed Brazilian for sure
lips painted and full,
European nose, black hair
falling to her breast

She does not say a word--
only looks and looks again
eyes open wide
easy in her native strength
and absolute silence
with me wondering
Who are you?

Six views I had
and each reflected
the same as the next.

Gentle sphinx,
your riddle remains
unanswered
and still I am alive
wondering
Who are you?

I will get no answer
but the question cannot be
unasked and it echoes
Who are you?
Who are you?
Who are you?

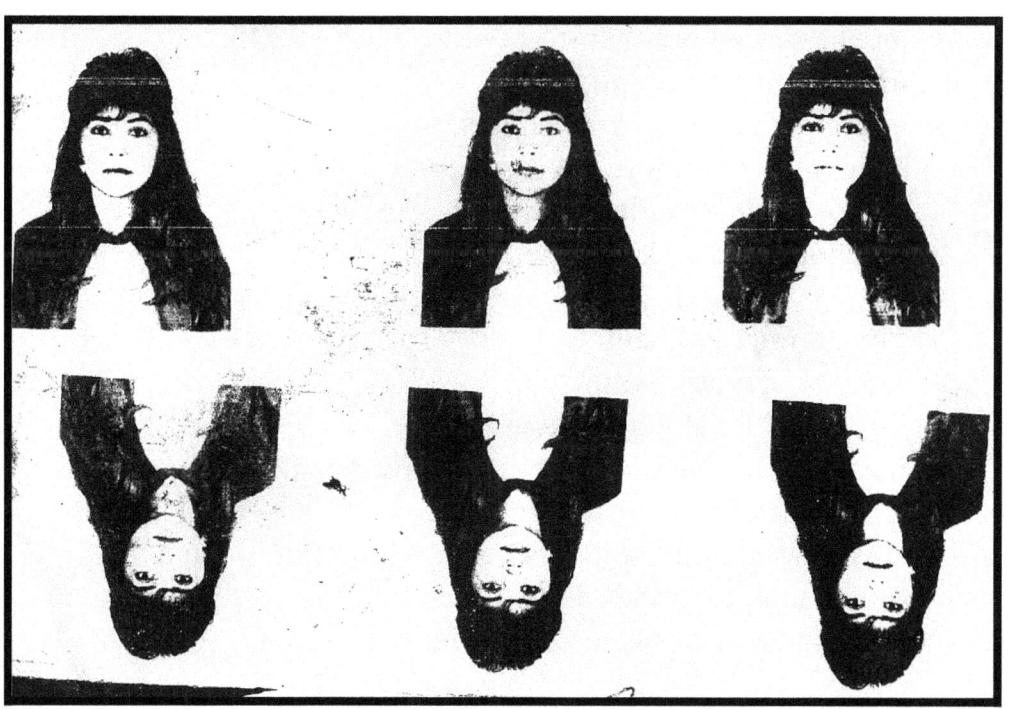

IV.

THE NIGHTMARE

> *Wander the awned streets....*
> *Might meet a robber or two.*
> *Well, meet him.*
>
> James Joyce
> *Ulysses*, Chapter 2

A Virgilian presence hovers at my left side,
as I meander an abandoned city,
the dark streets in the night-darkened Old City of Belém.
Gray pavements worn smooth by centuries of sluff and slog
seem to slide beneath our feet, one stone image after another.
(Flat stones had ballasted brave ships from the old stone world
to the new world of mud and mata.
The dead weight of Portugal became sidewalks in Grao Pará,
replaced in the hold with mahogany, amethyst, and guarana.)

Dodge the bus whose manifest reads: CANUDOS
the town at the end of the world.
Holes punctuate the narrow streets.
Lightening reveals more obscurity
in front of a white walled church,
its tall doors locked, its big bell silent.

Spatters of rain, palpably wet,
presage the pervasive rainfall
now lit lovely by streetlamps.
Shelter beckons under an awning at a deserted corner
but first I must open my umbrella.
Have you ever tried opening a collapsible umbrella in a dream?
The overhang provides a damp refuge
and the sight of a desolate Sea, curtained by rain.

A dark body,
neither African
nor Indian,
appears,
a white cloth slung
over bare shoulders.

He does not talk.
He does not greet.
He does not stay
but wavers away.

My guide perceives the visitor
in a tangle of his kind,
pointing here, delegating there….
"Truly, these are thieves of the night,
preparing their attack.
Now is the time for us to disappear."

I raise my hand
to summon a lone taxi.
A door opens.
We are gone.
    Ah, but this was no dream!
    Unlikely rescue
    from a nightmare
    came cheap that night--
    two bucks paid to a mute cabbie,
    saint of our salvation.

(The guide was an old friend of great wisdom, Diógenes Leal, who carries two wallets: one for himself and the other with $3 plus an assortment of boring business cards for thieves.)

REGULATIONS

(Found at VIDONHO'S HOTEL in Belém do Pará)

* The direction has the absolute right to prohibit the entrance of strange people or with doubtful aspect into the apartments and dependences of the hotel.

* The daily payment of the first day to be collected complete.

* In the exit day the daily finishes at 12:00 AM, if the flat have not being descupated until this time, the client has to pay a new daily payment.

* It's prohibited to put musical sounds in a loud volume.

* The bills have to be payd, in the moment apresented.

* If the clients don't pay the bills, they have to desocupate the apartment as per article of the law: 776, no. 1.778, and 779 of Civil Code.

* It's prohibited to extend clothes on the windows.

* It's prohibited children play in the hallway and salons.

* It's prohibited to throw out to the street papers or any thing.

* It's prohibited the presence of dogs or any kind of animal in the apartments.

* For the general tranquility, the lodgers must not make large noise in the apartments or in any dependence of the hotel.

Beers in Their Proper Order

Your normal Brazilian is very fond of beer, especially the cold ones, which is not surprising for such a hot climate. Here are some of the knicknames used for a single beer:

Uma cerveja—a beer
Uma bem gelada— a really cold one
Uma estupidamente gelada— a stupidly cold one
Uma veu de noiva—one veiled like a bride (frosted bottle)
Uma loura suada—a sweaty blonde (light colored beer with condensation dripping down the bottle.)
Uma canela de pedreiro—shins of the stone mason (frosted)
Uma perna do urubu—a buzzard's leg (which is white)
Um colorinho branco—one with a white collar (this for foam in the glass)
Uma do culhão do Penguin—one cold as a penguin's crotch
Aquella do Penguin—a polite way to say the one above

Then there is a certain order to the order beginning with:
1) *Uma cerveja, por favor.* (Or: *Uma loura suada, etc. por favor*)
2) *Mais uma*—one more
3) *Mais uma*
4) *Mais uma*
5-7?) *Mais uma…*
8) *Vamos tomar mais uma*—Let's have one more
9) *Saideira*—the "exit" out the door beer
10) *Expulsadeira*—the "expulsion" out the door beer
11) *Pe na bunda*—the kick in the ass out the door beer
12) If #11 does not do it, you are liable to the proprietor's *Pe-no-sacco.*

Nana's Recipe for Feijoada

Ingredients:
>   Enough *Charque* (salted beef)
>   Sufficient *Chorizo* (sausage)
>   Pork-back to taste
>   Pig foot
>   Pig ear
>   Bay leaf

(Soak all the above in water for 24 hours)

2 pounds of black beans (cleaned)

The way to prepare it:
>   Put the ingredients in a pot, cook until tender.
>   Add some tomato, onion, and greens

The way to serve it:
>   With rice, farofa, more greens, orange slices, and abobora (that's pumpkin to us).

Bom Apetite!

And don't forget the caipirnihas!

What I Like About Brazil (II)

All I did was ask where I could find a cup of coffee. I was in search of a quick fix before class – actually during class as I had left my English scholars of various aptitudes on remote control with an impromptu test to cover my absence. Their task: to read tough old Emily Dickinson's "I like to see it lap the miles, /And lick the valley up, / And stop to feed itself at tanks; / And then, prodigious, step…" Then there task would be to provide the poem with the title she had neglected to bestow. There I was stalking the campus after six o'clock with not a cafezinho vendor in sight. So I asked a man who was leaning against a post, "Por favor, *voce sabe onde eu posso descobrir um cafezinho?*" ("Please, can you tell me where I can find some coffee?") He roused himself from a sundown reverie, looked hither and yonder, then signaled me to follow him into a building, through a lobby, past the guard at the swinging door, by the air conditioned computers to his own office. He took a thermos from a cabinet and poured out a dose of black sugared coffee into a china demi-tasse. All this without a word. I drank it down on the spot, more Brazilian than American. Exactly the blast I was looking for. He smiled. I smiled. "*Obrigado, Senhor, e meus alunos agradecem voce também.*" ("Thank you, sir, and my students thank you as well.")

I found my way out of the maze and back to the classroom where I collected the tests and read the answers aloud: The Horse… The Galloping Horse… The Wild Horse… Every kind of horse but the Iron Horse. Then we moved on to other untitled riddles that resolved to snakes (*cobras*) and humming-birds (*beijaflores*—literally, "flower kissers").

Later on we entered the dashed field of her pain.

Por do Sol

sunset is a sudden death
with warning sufficient
only to regret
for a moment
the loss of a day

shadowed beings
replace men & women
defined no more
by a brash sun

life after death
is a residual force
diminishing
like a wave
no longer driven
by the wind

inevitable
the sleep in death
wakens images
borrowed
from day
then
from night
delivers
a sudden birth

TRANCE ARROWS

by
JAMES BOGAN

PORTUGUESE TRANSLATION
by
WALKYRIA MAGNO E SILVA

DESIGNS
EDWINA SANDYS

Begin as you go down the page white light bright around dark words only a sign towards something more indelibly marked

Trance Arrows

Some definitions of *trance*:

    trans-ire–to go across (Latin)

    the passage from life to death (12th century French)

    a state between sleeping & waking (1827)

    an exstasy or transportation of the Mind,
       which puts a man beside himself (1696)

    Time itself is but a short trance and we are carried
       Quickly through it. (1645)

Flechas do Transe

Algumas definições de *transe*:

    do latim *transire* – atravessar

    a passagem da vida Pará a morte (francês, séc. XII)

    estado entre o sono e a vigília (1827)

    êxtase ou estado da alma
        que coloca o homem lado a lado consigo mesmo (1696)

    O tempo não é mais do que um breve transe e nós somos
        celeremente levados através dele. (1645)

begin
as you go
down
the page
white
light
bright
around
dark
words
only
a sign
towards
something
more
indelibly
marked

comece
à medida em
que desce
a página
branca
clara
alva
cercando
palavras
escuras
apenas
um sinal
em direção a
algo
mais
indelevelmente
marcado

trance formation:

    breathe to balance
    open eyes closed
    every time a door

threshold meeting

    flee
    or follow
    through

trans(e)formação

   inspire
   equilibre
   olhos cerrados abertos

à porta

   no limiar
   fuja
   ou
   siga

    free

        space

           looms

              outward

                    free

           space

       opens

inward

      now

           coming

              together

                  the way

                      beyond

                    within

              dark

                far

                      shining

       espaço

           livre

              assoma

                  fora

             espaço

         livre

      abre

dentro

       agora

          junta-se

             em um

                a trilha

                   além

               é interior

            escura

               distante

                  reluzente

two strategies:

    seize
    open
    silence
    and wrestle
    the elusive
    stranger
    till he yields
    his name

    *****

    wait for him
    to appear
    in the next hour

duas estratégias:

    agarre
    o
    silêncio
    infinito/aberto
    e lute
    com o esquivo
    estranho
    até que ele libere
    seu nome

    *****

    espere que
    ele apareça
    na chegada hora

just listen

apenas ouça

a drum
beat with a bone
a rattle
made from a gourd
a feather
found by a spring
medicine
for the wayward
soul

um tambor
batido com osso
um chocalho
feito de cabaça
uma pluma
achada na fonte
cura
para um'alma
vagante

dream sleep
dream wake
dream sleep
dream wake

sono sonho
vigília sonho
sonhe sono
sonhe vigília

found
among
passing
sounds

passing
sounds

found
among
passing
sounds

achado
entre
sons
fugazes

fugazes
sons

achados
entre
sons
fugazes

```
sliding scales
    descent
        into
            notes
                strikes
                    fundamental
                        sparks of light
                            trancing day
                            from night
                                rising
                                    steps
                                        interval–
                                            filled
                                                with silence
                                                    and sound
                                                        alternate
```

  escalas
     escorregadias
       descem
         em
           notas
             tocam
               fagulhas luminosas
                 fundamentais
                   no transe do dia
                    desde a noite
                     suscitando
                      passos
                       cheios
                          de intervalos
                            de silêncio
                             e som
                               alternados

once

and again

the approach

repeated

an exercise

of grace

timed

to begin

only

when

it

does

uma vez

e mais uma

o rito

repetido

um exercício

de graça

marcado

Pará começar

apenas

quando

ele

começa

ascending

and

descending

along

the spine

spiral

waves

sound

clear

as

the

trumpet's

exacting

call

subindo

e

descendo

ao longo

da espinha

ondas

espirais

soam

claro

como

chamado

exato

de trompas

a distant boundry

not yet reached

the road of days

light & dark

divided

each kept

sound by dint

of effort applied

hourly

to an unknown

end

uma fronteira distante

ainda não alcançada

a estrada dos dias

claro e escuro

divididos

cada um

a salvo

por um golpe

de força

aplicada

de hora em hora

para um desconhecido

fim

Post-Trance Script

The *TRANCE ARROWS* sequence would like to be accompanied with a saxophone played by John Coltrane, Pharoah Sanders, or Iuri Guedelha. Failing that, the space-pauses could be made potent with measured silences. Clarence Wolfshohl of Timberline Press placed each leaded letter in its proper sequence in the original hand-pressed edition.

I had the great pleasure of the sustained collaboration of Walkyria Magno e Silva on the translation. She performed the impossible task of carrying poems from one language to another. During our extended debates, I ended up shifting several of the English words when the voyage into Portuguese indicated a better choice. We did arm wrestle over *flechas* and *setas* for arrows. *Setas* is more poetic but signifies a "projectile," as in a dart from a blowgun. Cupid and Caribes have *flechas* for their bows, so I held out for a *flecha*.

JB

Translator's Note

"Translate some poems?" asks James Bogan, once a professor of mine and now a welcome friend in our home. The idea grows and recalls some past experiences; but this is something bigger, deeper, with more responsibility attached to it. It will involve hours of unavailable time. It will reveal souls, visions... Yet, it has to be done and now is done: a fine experiment this stretching of minds so they are unable to go back to their original forms.

Walkyria Mango e Silva—Belém do Pará— 2006

BEYOND BELÉM

The Street of Thieves

Sandstone angels, arches, escutcheons, sculpted saints, scrolls, and foliage overrun the facade of the Church of St. Francis in Salvador, Bahia. It almost out-baroques Bernini. Four giant heads atop pillars glare prophetic into space, while a statue of the gentle saint of Assisi blesses those who enter the churchyard. The intricate pieces of this pious puzzle were shipped from Portugal in 1702 to be assembled in the New World of Salvador on the Bay of All Saints. Also built to last centuries was the antique street in front of the church. Foot-sized blocks of local granite, called *pedra bruta*, fit tightly together in a pattern of dizzying regularity that extend for narrow twisting miles. My mind winces at the thought of the racket iron-shod horses and iron-rimmed wheels must have made long ago, I am pulled out of my noisy reverie by a question from a ten year old boy sitting on a soccer ball:

"Are you from France?"

"No."

"Paraguay?"

"No."

"New Zealand?"

"No."

"Russia?"

"No."

"The United States?"

"Yes. Are you from Argentina?" I ask.

"No."

"Mozambique?"

"No."

"Portugal?"

"No."

"Bahia?"

"Yes. This man coming towards us now is a thief."

"How is it going?" the thief says in a pleasant tone.

"All swell. And you?" I reply.

"All swell. Be careful, this boy is a thief. He emphasizes the accusation with a twist of the thumb in the palm of his hand. This ubiquitous Brazilian gesture signifies robbery at its many levels be it on the beach at Copacabana, behind the post office, or in the governor's palace.

I take my leave of the pair and walk gingerly down the street that drops narrow between linked dwellings. My ankles split and splay over the rough cobbles. I feel a strange anxiety that I have walked myself into a rough spot that can only be walked out of by walking further. Oh, well.

At the first bend of a bent hairpin turn two boys are kicking a soccer ball across my path. The one with the "Self-Preservation" t-shirt tells me, "Lookout, there are thieves around the corner."

"Thank you for the warning but I must go this way to get to the port." He kicks the ball sharply to his friend who stops it on a dime, toes it up into the air, then shoots it back with his forehead.

I walk on down the street that now leads inexorably into the midst of a gang of boys. They are gathered for another sport: sledding down the incline on pieces of hard plastic. Zip. Zag. Zoom. It works.

As I pass, they talk among themselves, "Where does this American think he is going?"

To their surprise I respond, "I am going to the docks below.

Smiling happily one boy assures me, "You better look out. There is a thief at the bottom of the hill."

"What is the name of this thief, so I will know what to call him?" No one answers but they all laugh.

A lady appears at dim little shop and invites me in. Bags of sugar, bags of *farinha*, and tins of oil line the shelves. An old Singer sewing machine is in one corner and a square cooler makes a bar.

"Would you like a beer?"

"Actually I would like half a beer."

"Only large beers here."

"Some quinine water then."

"You know there are many thieves around here."

"So I have heard, but I must get to the port."

"I will send someone with you." She calls one of the boys into the shop and gives him the equivalent of a three dollar bill that she wants changed below.

Before setting out I address the multitude of fifteen gathered around the door, "You all better look out! Perhaps it is I who am the thief," as I make to bop the boy on the head and snatch the money; however, nobody takes me for the Artful Dodger.

My three-foot bodyguard and I reach the bottom of the hill without incident except for the offer of some marijuana from behind a barred window. Further on two guys lurk in an alley but are too busy with no good to notice us. My escort peels off on his own errand as I proceed unmolested beyond the Street of Thieves, having been guided by what phalanx of angels and haunted by what Devils, God only knows.

BEYOND TURVANIA

I.

To get to Gustavo's *fazenda*, first drive south out of Goiania, the million person capital of Goiás. In ten miles the scene goes from the urban high rises and graffitied garage doors to pastoral rolling hills and fog bedraped hummocks. All green. Until it gets really dark this side of Turvania—*Onde o Futuro é Agora!* ("Where the Future Is Now!"). And if that is so, then our future is going to be a lot quieter in the future.... Two locals confirm our handwritten directions.... Yes, take that road and look for the placard that says Fazenda Veneto. Lightning bounces from cloud to cloud, after-shocks of the afternoon's thunderous rain. Fazenda Veneto. Now look for the NEXT right... onto the dirt road with the occasional mud warp. I whistle a steady minimalist whistle to keep us going, a tactic that works in the Ozarks usually and here too, for the time being. Keep going, till you get to the BIG HOLE, and drive down into it. Note well: Maintain your momentum or you will not make it up the slippery slope and out the other side, which opens, or rather closes, into a straight red dirt road, fringed by miles of green sugar cane. For cachaça? "No, for ethanol." Six owls, little ones, flap and swoop out of sight. "Plenty of rodents, plenty of snakes for them to eat." The fringed walls of cane give way to pasture and woods: GUSTAVO'S FAZENDA. Fazenda São Bento.

Along the Brazilian version of an Ozark two-track, we drive on, eventually to a lane that takes us through the dark to the original farm house, now appended to a comfortable double porched house, tricked out in tile. We are here. Nothing to it. Applause for Marcos, the pilot, from Felipe the seven year old and his older brother of nine, Gabriel. I walk into the house asking in a loud voice, "*Terra Del Fogo? Nesta direção??*" ("Is this the way to Tierra del Fuego?") Such an out of the dark inquiry coming from a certified gringo in the middle of nowhere in the middle of the night causes an understandable consternation among the assembled friends. At this moment Gustavo appears as his piratical self of long hair and formidable physique and saves me an awkward moment with an introduction: "Jim Bogan, Meester Jim Bogan..."

I follow him to the old peasant house next door, to the enormous kitchen with two wood fire ovens going. The ceiling is patinaed totally black with a century or two of smoke. Oven domes of fire hardened red clay sprawl halfway across the large room. One kindling-fueled fire heats a wok-like iron pan for scorching meat, another for baking bread. We join the rest of the family at a long wood table. Cold beer after cold beer appears and disappears.... Under the tutelage of Benedito, the brother-in-law, my vocabulary grows: *empapuçado*—full up. A batch of kids joins Felipe and Gabriel. Thirteen year old Osvaldo speaks clear and colloquial English. "Yeah." We move to the veranda for dinner: lamb, rice, beans, beer. The lamp lit house is wrapped around in a profound *escuridão*--a velvet dark murkiness.

Lots of diverse talk is sparked by Rosangela's and Gustavo's shared daughters:

Ana is reading Proust's *Memoir du Temps Perdue*.
Maria is reading Baudelaire's *Fleurs du Mal*.
Clarice is reading Aldous Huxley's *Doors of Perception*.

Lordy.

So I introduce William Blake into the discussion, who donated that last title... and Clarice instructs me in turn on the virtues of Argentine Malbec from the Valley of Turangato. A thousand miles away in Rio de Janeiro, Carnival is in full carnal swing, while I feel like a visiting courtier in some latter day Shangri-la of civilized discourse. In Salvador, Bahia, half the population is in a trance and the other half is drunk. They are dancing in the streets. There is no street here but the conversation turns quadrilles of grace and I am a stranger at home, awash in Portuguese, under the local tutelage of Professor Brahma, a pretty good beer, when Gustavo offers to upgrade me with some *Pinga*.... *Pinga* is another name for *cachaça*, a cane alcohol which is cheap and potable when bought from the store and mixed down with fresh lime, sugar, and ice for a *caipirinha*. On the other hand, it is often as harsh as low grade white lightning... He pours me a shot glass full and it is dark brown. *Macaco Velho*, brown as an "Old Monkey." Commercial *cachaça* is every bit as clear as vodka. I ask no questions but sip it. Oh my goodness... Are you sure this is pinga? They laugh at me... It tastes like a really good cognac, VVVSOP, and it is strictly family. This spirit has been aged for more than thirty years in three kinds of wood: *Balsamo*—for its aromatic properties, *Amburana*—for its medicinal tang, and *Jatobá*—a powerful hard wood. The containers *toneis*-"tuns"—are nine feet high tapering to twelve feet and each holds more than 3000 liters. They dwell just over the hill at the old *engenho*. I never met a "homebrew" of this quality before. It tastes good. It is smooth. It feels good. A guy could drink pinga, if this was what *pinga* was like. So I drink some more of Gustavo's *pinga* slowly, slowly--treat it like that very good cognac. This *pinga* cannot be bought. You have to not get lost, not get stuck in the mud somewhere in the middle of Goyaz.... And be a pal of the Fazendeiro...

The next day I wake up--without a hangover, I might defensively add--and actually see where I am in this veranda-ed home, shaded by huge mangoes and bordered by a diverted stream. A lanky *siriema*, a crested bird of ivory and grey and brown, the size of a watermelon on sticks, deliberately galumphs through the grass ready to swallow a snake, thus working this wild garden like a New World peacock. One edge of the yard is lined out in a sturdy fence of vertically planted logs. A pond full of fish and good for a swim is just out of sight beyond a fringe of prodigious bamboo.

An expedition is in the works... a hike to the Rio Turvo. A group of twelve starts off. I am geared up in summer Ozark style: river shoes, plastic pants (i.e., nylon), long sleeved cotton shirt of blue, sunglasses, sunblocked, Offed, non-descript brimmed hat and a backpack loaded with unusual stuff. Gustavo has even found me a *cajado* of bamboo for a walking stick. The pasture we are walking through could pass for a chunk of Phelps County, with its clumpy grass and spikey plants. Two people turn back, already a bit ripped about the ankles. We trudge on in a line, the boys keeping up at first but soon becoming dubious about the pleasures of eluding, and the pains of not eluding, wicked thorns. Me too. The blatant sun broils the expeditionaries.

Then we meet a herd of black buffalo, who clear out as one in a rumble. Onward. Red dirt termite domes, *cupinzeiros*, punctuate the pasture like miniature ruins from Angor Wat. The occasional black and white hawk swoops by. It is hot. It is getting hotter. The boys feel chumped, which brings to mind several too long hikes I unwittingly imposed on my kids. I can still see Jesse, a bit irate at four, putting one dogged foot in front of the other on some outlandish foray. Marcos hoists Felipe onto his shoulders and I join Gabriel in kicking our walking sticks in unison and cursing in two languages. He also speaks a very effective and colloquial English. "Damn heat. *Puta merda*. Damn heat. *Puta merda*"—in time with kicking the stick. Unexpectedly the pasture gives way to the shade of the forest—or jungle. It looks foresty to me. *Floresta*. A trail wanders off into it. Gustavo confers with Marcos and disappears into the woods. Marcos points a way to the river and everybody's spirits rise as we are shaded from the brutal sun and now we are walking easily through a scrubby forest.

"Let me have the machete," says Marcos and I turn around so he can extricate it from the pack. He trots off the trail and chop chop chop comes back with a pineapple. Wild. Smallish. VERY SWEET, and slightly seedy. This jungle gift revives everybody's spirits, including my dubious ones. We forge ahead bearing always to the west and eventually there is a sound like the wind, but it is the river and then it is gone--like the wind. The trail leads on and on. Finally, a tan swirl flows through the trees. Rio Turvo could be translated as Turbid River, and its caramel waters are suffused with earth. I guess the current is running eight miles an hour, but it would have to be recalculated into kilometers here (13?). We edge down a shore as be-brushed as any in the Arkansas Ozarks. I am the first one in the water. Osvald's mother is really fearful of the current--with good reason: next stop Buenos Aires, but there is a backwash here and it is so refreshing after being parboiled on the hike. All the guys get in and hang from various limbs. The water is moving too fast to interest any vicious snake. The kids slip off from the limbs and swim towards me, away from the current and I gather them in with my bamboo stick and general shouting to increase the sense of danger—and care. Nobody is looking forward to the walk back. Nobody. And we don't have to because here comes Gustavo in his capacious pickup to take us back, but not before he gets to jump into the turbid waters of the racing Rio Turvo.

Back at the Fazenda there is time for a bit of sumo wrestling on the platform in the pond, before settling in for some serious hammock meditations. I do not recall much after that, maybe a dream about a quiet past in a slow rhythm hard to find this side of paradise.

I wake up to a whooping. Most of the company has decamped to the modern world while I dreamt, but here comes Andre, who is as massive as a medium-sized giant, whooping and laughing and displaying a sizable *tucunaré* he has just pulled out of the pond. Dinner for eight. He is a big Brazilian of German and Italian extraction, a serious chef and a man of good sense. His wife, Lea, is as petite as he is huge and they display a refreshing constant of affection that is more common amongst Brazilians than any other culture I have dwelt with. Andre goes off to cook the exotic *tucunaré*.... I am not much of a fish person but I like a fresh *tucunaré* as much as the next *caboclo*. I remember the first time I had *tucunaré* in the Amazon and how surprised I was at its fresh taste.... I returned to the Ozarks and among my tall tales of the Amazon was of the quality of their incomparable *tucunaré*, a word marvelous to pronounce.... It was on my next trip to Belém that I actually saw a live *tucunaré*.... Damn, but that *tucunaré* sure looks like a large mouth bass. "It is a large mouth bass..." And Andre has a veritable lunker of a *tucunaré* in hand, in pan, in oven....

Before dinner there are more discussions about football and grammar (another, lesser known, Brazilian pastime) sparked with doses of *Pinga Própria*. Gustavo promises that tomorrow he will show me the *engenho* where the concoction continues to mature. At thirty it seems quite wise to me. That *tucuare* did not die in vain by the way. It went out in grand but simple style, the center of one more riot of conversation.

After a slow take-off roll the next morning, we jumped into two vehicles--Andre, Gustavo and I in the pickup and Marcos with the boys in his car to check out the *engenho*, the old sugar works over the hill. We went through two gates with "Ozark latches," a detachable pole with three strands of wire, secured and unsecured by wire loops at top and bottom. We drive by a wood fenced corral, down a two track towards a white stone house with two enormous vultures perched like black angels on a dead tree at corner of the structure....

The old iron sugar press rose red above the waist-high grass. Made in Scotland. For decades and decades and decades peasants fed this cogged and wheeled machine enough sugar cane to loop the planet in a tube of sweetness. Some of it was fermented in the vats inside the small building. I was quite curious to see the huge containers. I had a profoundly ulterior motive in this. We followed Gustavo towards the door. An immense dirt dauber nest enveloped one corner of the building. I stalled in my steps to gawk at the organic structure, when Gabriel started to yip and flap. Marcos urged him to keep calm: "*Calma*," calmly. Some dang black bug, a batch of them, got in our hair. Clumped on Gabriel's back. I scattered them with my hat. They were aggravating, not biting, but then I was bitten, not by the irritating bug, but by a bee...two… Gabriel now had reason to yip, to scream... Marcos got him running towards the car... and the boy screamed as he ran.

I took off towards Gustavo's truck in a forty yard dash that probably eclipsed my personal best record and sat in the truck for a shaky minute, but the electric windows were down and enraged bees were on patrol. They were going to find me.... I retreated further to Marcos' car and joined him and Gabriel, who was doing his best now not to give in to fright and pain. I started in with the only thing I know: Okay, Gabriel, breathe slowly and deeply. Again: *Respira, lente, profunda, de novo lente, profunda...* breathe deeply and slowly again.... He did.

Marcos was distracted with fear for Felipe who was cut off in the old building with Gustavo and Andre. Marcos had been bitten dozens of times.... I recalled seeing him flailing, trying to protect Gabriel and check out Felipe's whereabouts at the same time, when at a run he shepherded Gabriel to the car.... I began on Marcos: "Breathe, slowly, deeply. Just do this. There is nothing else to do. Breathe slowly and deeply." Marcos' pain was compounded by not knowing what had become of Felipe. I said," If anything bad had happened we would have heard more screams...." Cold comfort.

His color was off. He was sweating a dark sweat, but consciously breathing slowly, deeply. Marcos is one tough character, so it was unnerving to hear him say, "*Não estou bem.*" "I am not well." Breathe.... We put the car seat back... He breathed. Later he told me spots of light appeared in his field of vision and they amplified out till everything was an undifferentiated bright brilliance. He continued to breathe slowly and deeply. His heart rate slowed some. His respiration had tightened up, but he continued to breathe slowly, deeply.

Gustavo, Andre, and Felipe finally showed up... They had been trapped inside the house by the swarm of maddened bees looking for trouble. Felipe had looked up to the ceiling to discover hundreds of black fruit bats hanging upside down waiting for the dark... He was not exactly amused but he noted them well. He saw the enormous barrels full of aged *pinga*.... Eventually they went out another door and found us in Marcos' car....

Marcos seemed somewhat more stabilized, but his body's reaction to the bees' poison was still going on and whether to go to the fazenda or to the hospital was in the balance. Gustavo got behind the wheel and I followed with Andre, closing the Ozark latches behind us... At the crossroads, Marcos decided to go back to the fazenda. He was not well, but he was less worse.

Gustavo opened up his first aid chest but Marcos took a pass on the quasi-lethal antidote for *jararaca* bites. I came up with a couple of anti-histamines from my back pack. He drank a lot of water. Rosangela washed the bites with alcohol. His vision was much improved though blurred at the edges and there was still a knot in his chest. We walked slowly down to the small waterfall where the diverted stream dropped off into the pasture.... The clear water brought him back. He threw up once, twice, thrice, the body doing its own thorough work to clean itself out. We sat down on the veranda and watched Marcos out of the collective corners of our eyes as he breathed slowly and deeply in the hammock. He was going to be okay.

So who was the luckiest of all today? I opined it was Marcos, because for the all the bad luck of the attack, his ample constitution was enormous good luck and with this naturopathic shock treatment, maybe he would never get arthritis or rheumatism! On a more conventional level it was Felipe, to give a positive swing to this just-short-of-traumatic experience. He had been rewarded with the rare sight of hundreds of fruit bats hanging above the ancient tuns of *Pinga*. Nor did he suffer one bite....

We drank beers. Marcos swung slowly in the hammock. Andre allowed as how the *pinga* was surely well protected with such a ferocious guard. We drank off the last of the Irish whiskey I had imported from the United States in my flask--for snake bite and against frost bite. Gustavo filled the flask from the *Pinga Própria* bottle in the Fazenda. Marcos got up and claimed he was okay, no headache, breathing normal, a bit bleary around the edges but okay.

We got in the car and headed back to Goiana in no great rush, stopping at the crossroads to talk with Fé, a ninety-year-old man of "diminished capacity," looked after for years by Gustavo's family. He is a gnomish guy, not much taller than a fire plug. We shook hands and I told him I had traveled around Cape Horn and into the interior of Brazil to meet him, and in a way I had, so I asked him if he had any messages for the people of the United States. He laughed and laughed, understanding somehow this outrageous claim and he looked me in the eye and from very far away he said very clearly: *"CUIDADO."* BE CAREFUL.

We shook hands. Marcos drove us out through the Sugar Cane Alley, traversing the big hole, which was not quite as terrifying in the daylight, but still capable of swallowing an automobile. Back through Turvania "Where the future is now!" Back on the highway, back to the present. With care.

II.

Two years later I was back beyond Turvania, where the future had not changed much, but a lot had changed at the Fazenda São Bento. Rosangela, Gustavo's endearing wife, had died of a vicious cancer some months ago. The daughters were stashed in various cities. The bounty of personnel was elsewhere this Carnival season, which was for Gustavo, Marcos, and me more of a retreat. Discussions about dreams, disappointment, and adventures intermingled.

Marcos came up with the idea of making a canoe trip on the Rio Turvo to explore the twenty mile run from the edge of Turvania to the Fazenda São Bento. That sounded fantastic to me based on numerous voyages in the past on various rivers with these guys. Gustavo himself had never made the trip. To rest up we spent the day dreaming dreams and disputing Portuguese grammar from three hammocks. Gerund or participle? My old Latin teacher, Father North, would have known. The next day we set off for the exploration of the RioTurvo with three paddles and a large box of cold beer.

The river was up some with a noticeable, but not furious current; and it was turbid as befits its name. We launched the green *Canoa Canadense* with Gustavo in the stern, Marcos at the bow, and me in the Cleopatra seat claiming that I would be "intelligent ballast." It took a wobbly while for us to find our collective balance.

Rio Turvo was a lot like the mighty Little Piney, but muddier. I would note that the locals in Phelps County, Missouri, consider the Little Piney fool's work in a canoe, but apt for the more agile kayak. The Ozark discipline of doing nothing but float, guided by minimalist ruddering, was not of much use because the sharp turns were festooned with numerous tree tangles to get through. Intermittent stretches of the river were unobstructed—until the next turn.

So here we are doing the work of fools in good faith, figuring out the best tactics for the day, while all the time scanning the scene for Blue Morpho butterflies, the *jaburu* (a huge heron-like bird with a big black beak and a red scarf), monkeys, and there there there a flight of Toucans overhead. Ah, the joys of a Brazilian float trip!

BUT, in our haste to get onto the river we neglected to inspect the boat. Water. Inside the boat, not outside where it is supposed to stay. There was a leak. ("Ah, but it is only a tiny hole…") I must say that I really prefer a dry boat. In the Ozarks in winter it is really important, if you don't want to freeze a toe off, but here on a warm day, it is only a nuisance. "We can fix it." There are not many places to "pull over" as the current slides quickly between seriously overgrown banks. Marcos spots what looks to me like a rock ledge of three feet. It is a rock ledge of three feet and apparently one of the only places we can stop. And we do, tossing the gear into the jungle and then in a "Dance on a Small Rock," with twister-like choreography, we managed to turn the boat over on its back and wedge it against the shore. The "small hole" was really not so small, but my two ingenious friends stuffed the opening with a plastic sack, taped it over, then sealed it with the fire from a lighter. We drank a beer perched on the rock ledge and shoved off again. No leaks.

Immediately in front of us was a multi-layered net of vines hanging across the river. I estimate now the vegetal strings, ropes, and hawsers were three deep—vertical, horizontal, and diagonal. The difficulty was compounded by a tree trunk with curling branches below. All three of us have spent a lot of time in canoes, and this inescapable challenge required the skills of a lifetime to confront. I kept the balance, Gustavo steered, and Marcos grabbed a branch and another branch. One of the branches snatched my hat. We pulled our way through hand over hand successfully without turning over. The only real problem was THE THORNS. "Ahiyee. Youch. *Puta Merda*." Worse. We were floating again. My hat caught up to us.

"Well, that was a bit rough. Why all the thorns?" It was explained to me that where the lands along the river had been deforested some time ago, great jungle trees had been replaced by ambitious low-life plants, a lot them with thorns. "That one has a name: '*Volta Aqui Meu Bem*…. Come Back Here, My Dear'" and you do because your shirt, your hat, your ear is attached. The only good thing I can say about the plant is that thorns are short, sort of like the multi-flora rose which I have extirpated from my own lands, except for one bush used for teaching purposes alongside a patch of likewise educationally purposed poison ivy.

Anyway, that was pretty awful but we escaped it, until the next bend and the next veil of thorns. "*Aich. Ooch. Puta Merda*." Worse. We got through but that time the spiked gauntlet drew blood. I do not doubt that Teddy Roosevelt went through similar flesh rips as he descended the River of Doubts a hundred years ago.

We floated about two hundred yards unmolested and a gang of green parrots talked their own language back and forth in a tree. A fabulous racket. Another curve and another veil of thorns. This time we were tripped up and turned over in hand to thorn combat with the plants. Under the water I had a vision of the sun, filtered brown. I had escaped the creepy thorns. As we were swept downstream, we herded paddles, beer box, and canoe together. Eventually we managed to find a hospitable mud shore at which to reassemble ourselves. Knee deep mud gives way to ankle deep mud. Good enough. Marcos and Gustavo tend the canoe in the shallows thinking correctly that it is not worth the trouble to pull the boat onto the mud. I peer into the jungle. An enormous termite nest bulges out from the ringed trunk of a palm tree. Green and brown vegetation goes further than I can see, when a biggish bird about the size of pileated peckerwood flits into and out of and into view: A luminous crimson crest atop a black body streaked with white. It is a third cousin of our Ozark woodpecker.

The boat is ready and so are we. At the next curve at no great surprise and some genuine disappointment is another veil of thorns. This time we are stuck broadside against a tree limb and there is Gustavo behind me totally horizontal and immobilized—crucified by branches of thorns. He cannot move. We must move. Very delicately I lift some branches. "Ouch, *Puta Merda*." Worse. He is released and so are we for the time being. I try to console him for his bloody legs, torn shorts, and scratched nose. "Jesus only had to bear with a crown of thorns, you got the full suit."

I am wondering how far we have gone in this supposed trip of twenty miles… With three hours in and six hours of daylight to go, we are maybe a third of the way with countless wicked warps of thorns to go. I ask if the river is likely to open up. Actually it is going to get more *fechado*… I have been a full dues paying member on disastrous expeditions before. The thought of flailing our way through these jungle barricades IN THE DARK gives me, uh, pause. Is there any way out of here? The real jungle (*mata, selva, floresta*-- call it what you will) is two miles thick and then gives way to three miles of pasture. Let's go a bit further. The sky is a friendly blue inhabited by soft white clouds that make me wish I was a kite or a *jaburu*.

At the next thorn trap, Marcos just jumps out of the boat and guides it through the mess of limbs and thorns. At the next one, we ALL jump out and float downstream. Sometimes you could walk on the sandy bottom; sometimes you would be tripped up underwater by branches. One small but comforting thought: Since the current is so strong, alligators are unlikely to bother us. Oh good.

We stopped at another mud bank to drink a beer and eat a ham and cheese sandwich. Marcos smoked. I allowed as how I was probably the only gringo in the history of the world to picnic here. Seems likely. White herons, almost as big as the Great Blue Herons of the Ozarks, sail by in squadron.

Again in the boat with Marcos at the stern now, Gustavo in the water, and me in the front, we anxiously paddle downstream. It is hard not to wince in advance at the thought of what is just around the next bend. No surprise: an embassy of "Come Back Here, My Dear" awaits our arrival. This time I catch it at speed across the face and make an instantaneous decision: ABANDON SHIP. The water is a blessed relief and I am pleased upon surfacing to discover both of my eyes are in their customary sockets, only now outlined in a clownish red.

Two of our three paddles are gone gone. And my hat, gone. We are barely halfway, if Gustavo can be believed--and he has never made the trip before. The conditions can only get worse, not better. There is a screech from the woods that is probably not that of a panther. Too early for the panther. Later.

"Well, this is another trip I won't forget, but I am NOT complaining."

Before flipping over again, which is going to be soon, we spot an actual campsite along the river, i.e., a circle of rocks and some burnt wood. At this simple sign of human use, we lug the boat into the woods. The decision is made in seconds in unanimous acclamation: Let's just walk out.

Never have I been so pleased to walk across a swamp (*brejo*). And after that the lone cow-trudged path seems a veritable wonder of civilized engineering and eventually it leads to the edge of a pasture. In the fair distance is a desolate shed. In the foreground is a cow. We are almost saved. Two sandals lie orphaned in the middle of the path. Weird. We walk. Dogs bark. Three scratched-bloody men, one carrying a paddle, arrive at the house in the middle of nowhere. It is as real as a picture: a white porticoed veranda surrounds the farm house. In a blue hammock suspended in the late afternoon floats old the half-sick Fião, a neighbor of Gustavo from two Fazenda's over. We had made it about half way as it turned out. Gustavo announces himself: "Gustavo." Fião responds with Gustavo's full name: "Gustavo Carneiro Silva Faz." The old man is amused, but does not treat us as though we have arrived from outer space. He is the angel of our salvation. In short order we are sitting in his car—and never has the back seat of a compact Fiat felt so first class—on our way back along several red dirt roads to the far side of Turvania, where…. He drops us off at a taxi line of one taxi and we are soon headed back to Fazenda São Bento, meterless.

In a cricket-like score of scratches made to branches broken, the thorns won a lopsided victory: 358-24, not to mention the trashing of Gustavo's shorts, my blue shirt, and Marcos' credibility. Afterwards we counted our blessings:

1) Though there are bloody scratches and sharp gouges distributed among us, they are all only flesh wounds.

2) We escaped the clutches of the Rio Turvo at the only place where we would not have let ourselves in for worse:

3) We were not caught out in the dark, on the river, in the jungle, super-slashed by invisible thorns of the night. Worse.

It was a great trip in some ways, and certainly one that banished all existential woes in the misery of the moment. There was even some talk of how we were lucky to deal with *Volta Aqui Meu Bem*, rather than the more truculent thorns of the Ozark locust tree which, not only punctures more deeply into the skin, but leaves a broken point likely to fester later.

Croquet anyone?

Four More Poems

I.

Sad Anthony

I never saw a painted saint
so preoccupied, Portinari,
til I knelt before
your worried San Antônio.
Clad in brown robes
he walks a blue road
that fades white
in the distance of the plain,
the same that swells
beyond the edge
of your hometown
out the windows of this church.
A purple hump of hill
holds the horizon
in the painting as well.
Just what cares
you settled
on his vexed brow
I don't know
but his face
reflects
problems of this
not another
world.
Shuttered eyes
cast down
but tranced in

he stands
pressed
beyond mortal relief
and deaf
to the divine
chiding
of the doomed
child secure
in his large hands;
"But, Tonho, don't you see…"

Not yet he doesn't
and in this, Candido,
you keep
the saint human.

* Candido Portinari (1903-1962) was born in Brodosqui, State of São Paulo, Brazil, of Italian immigrant parents. The painting of St. Anthony is in a little chapel aross from his family home. The usual iconography of St. Anthony has the Christ-child in his arms. St. Anthony is the patron saint of marriage and of finding lost objects like wallets and souls.

II.

Not Included in the Official Report:

From the window of a slowed cab at the foot of Christo Redemptor
I note the trademark on the cartop carrier: *Long Life*

>Beyond a stopped car
>the too still body
>face down flat on the pavement
>a teenage girl or boy it was
>
>the red blood running dry to the curb
>the distance kept by the semi-circular crowd
>the emptiness in the air
>the too still body
>all whisper "dead"

as the cab accelerates
                and the driver crosses himself

III.

What I Did Not Buy from Strolling Vendors on the Beach at Copacabana in One Hour

sunglasses, sand darts, chicklets, or wristlets
red plastic toucans or a stuffed piranha
the "Order and Progress" t-shirt flag of Brazil
a lace table cloth or genuine emeralds (not really)
Marlboros or a map of Manhattan

a bottle of *caipirnha* (white lightening)
    with whole pears in it somehow
two black-faced puppets dancing on a string
color photos of Sugar Loaf, Christo Redemptor,
    or the Girl from Ipanema
genuine emeralds (really)

What I did buy:

Two good beers and roasted peanuts, cone-wrapped in newspaper.

IV.

In the Heart of the Jungle of Stones

The guitarist strums the strings of a common guitar
with long fingers swaying his folk song out the interior
into strong chords of sound
 His back rests against a twisted tree
and he sings as much to sing
as to say.
A batch of Brazilians complete his circle
in a subdued but accurate chorus
this Sunday afternoon in a São Paulo Park..

The boy has a mismatched face Picasso dreamt up:
      black thatch hair,
      pitch-dark eyes
      somehow harmonized
      across different planes,
      cheekbones as indicative
      as brown fingers.
      A clown-wide mouth broadcasts
      searing melodies through
      two lines of white teeth.

It is the treacherous tremolo
that catches me
as I wander past,
catches me unaware
catches me unprotected
and drops me
into a forgotten well
of healed pain.

Some words resolve into meaning
out of a blur of sound:
    triste--sad
    dormindo--sleeping
    amorada--lover
    solzinho--alone
But the knife that cuts into my subtle heart
is a wobbling tone ancient as tribal chant
yet first cousin to the South-side blues

In the mudbrick cafe
behind me
a fire leaps
from coals
to ceiling--
a billow of flame.

I did not know
I was so alive
to suffer so.

It is something
short of *banzo*,
the lethal nostalgia
of an uprooted African slave
and something
more than
the lingo-centrically
untranslatable
saudades,
this unbidden
untraceable
longing.
      Let the poem be the translation.

BEYOND UPPER PARADISE

I certainly liked spending time with the gang from Goiania, a forest friendly, daring, expert group of guys who had been around the bend, so to speak. Many years ago, Fabão, who had done a stint as a professional basketball player in France, before becoming a professional hotelier on the edge of the jungle, was talking about his scheme to buy a chunk of property even further out than where he was already. Way further out. He described the place as bio-diverse in the extreme. It had everything: A thousand different trees, including the *angico*, the fragrant *balsamo*, and *mangueira*, which is a mango to us; hundreds of kinds of birds, including toucans, the watchful *bem-te-vi*, Martin Pescador, and heronsheronsheronsherons; dozens of beasts, including *anta* the anteater, *quati* the raccoon, and *onça* the jaguar; roughly half a gazillion of bugs, including a million fireflies (*vagalumes*).

"Does it have snakes?" I interrupted.

"Lots of snakes," he replied merrily. "Anacondas. Poisonous ones, too. *Jararaca, Cascavel* the Rattler. The place is by the Rio Preto and near a waterfall without a real name and what is more, there is no road, only a trail."

Of course, I was intrigued. "So where is it?"

"Beyond Upper Paradise." He was not kidding. Alto Paraiso is a town 150 miles north of Brasilia and his desired domain was somewhere the other side of that. To keep a short story short, I threw in some cash along with a couple of other shareholders and joined a consortium to buy the land. I did not know if I would ever get there myself, but the price was in the hundreds (of dollars) and I figured, perhaps my heirs could use a bolt hole in Brazil. Perhaps I could use a bolt hole in Brazil. Furthermore, it would be worth it in bar-talk to be able to boast a holding in central Brazil with all the qualities mentioned above. I was in.

How legal the papers would be was debatable, but I did not bother to debate. I visited Goiás a couple more times over the years and received reports that the corners of the property had been marked; that Fabão had spent several nights there several times; that two hammock hooks had been screwed into tall trees for the eventual day I would actually get there to hang my own hammock and enjoy the sun and rain. There was never time to get an expedition launched during my visits and I was happy enough to make due with the River of Thorns.

So back in Missouri when colleagues mentioned time-shares in New Orleans, a vacation on the Isla Mujeres, or even a cruise through the Greek Islands, I could always drop my "beyond Upper Paradise" card, as though it were a trump. Selden Trimble, a bourbon-dipped chess master, was particularly skeptical: "You have never seen the place??? Have you not heard of Florida land schemes? I bet they have them in Brazil."

"Well, I have seen pictures and there was even a thatched hut. Lots of trees for sure. And a river that may inundate part of the land in the rainy season."

"And you have a deed?"

"Well, actually no. Fabão has what papers there are, I think. But he is trustworthy guy. Pal of mine. Like you. Last time I was there, I stayed at his lodge, fitted out with a hammock on the edge of the jungle. He would not let me pay any rent, but I insisted on throwing a couple hundred bucks more at our holding for taxes or upkeep or whatever."

"And you think you own this place???" Selden skepticized.

"Yeah, I am part of the group. My heirs can hide out there, if the Canadians invade. I don't know if I will ever get there myself. So far I have settled for trips down thorny rivers and skirmishes with angry bees. But maybe you would like to spend a weekend there? Fabão has a chess board. I am sure I could arrange it. But bring your hiking boots, as our terrain is a couple of miles off the nearest rutted road. The trail is said to be well maintained."

"You are crazy."

"No, I am not."

******

Getting to get there ain't easy, but here it is:

Let's say you are in Brasilia, the jet-plane shaped capitol of Brazil, carved out of the state of Goiás in 1961 into a federal district, like Washington, DC. The city's foundation is embedded in a subterranean band of crystal. Brasilia is not very Brazilian in its geometric layout and poured cement architecture, but behind the standardized facades of its many plazas you can walk through a door and enter any of Brazil's 26 states, from Amazonas to Rio Grande de Sul, from Acre to Sergipe and meet the locals and eat their regional food. Try an Amazon favorite, a bowl of *açaí* mixed with tapioca, then drive North about three hours. Traffic dissipates to almost nothing in twenty minutes and four fast lanes shrink to two lumpy ones. The land stretches out like Wyoming without the snowy mountains. All green now in March, the landscape will be burnt brown by June. Outside the town of Alto Paraiso, pick up centrifugal force on the roundabout and swing west. Now it is about 20 miles further through a weird landscape of undulating plain landmarked with cone-like hills and whale-like mountains, like the one called *Baleia*—"The Whale." The vista here is oft photographed—not so much as the Redemptive Jesus, arms outstretched over poor Rio de Janeiro—but this view is the icon of Brazilian emptiness, preserved as a National Park with some draconian rules, such as: no one is allowed inside its 250 square miles. The asphalt abruptly gives way to hard packed red dirt trenched by recent rains, which inspires the driver to increase his speed to 90 kilometers an hour. Whoever has the shock absorber concession in this county must do a great business. Slow down for the hamlet of São Jorge. Buy a bottle of local cachaça, AGED THREE MONTHS! with sticks of *bálsamo* added for flavor. Keep going, making multiple choices bearing left and right or right and left. When in doubt, take the rougher roadway. Turn right at the thatched bus stop, and proceed at a greatly reduced speed until reaching the flooded river. Stash the car in the jungle.

There are three of us: my friend Marcos, Marcio who knows the way, and me armed with a walking stick. We hoist our heavy packs in unison and step warily into the turbid stream, which is supposed to be shallow, but the bottom is lined with rocky ankle breakers and the current is swift. We edge across the swift current—waist-deep at times—and have almost reached the other side when Marcos slips and in a fraction of a second I can see him—and most of our food—headed for the Amazon; but he grabs the stick I have planted on the bottom and saves himself—along with most of our food.

With the echo of Bob Marley in my head about just how many rivers we have to cross, we reach the further shore and continue along the "good trail" promised for the ultimate two mile trek. The sun, waning but brilliant, filters through the forest. Soon we come upon an adobe brick house, thatched with local palm. Seu João and his wife Dona Amelia have lived here for the best part of 40 years, running some cattle and presiding over a batch of chickens, most of whom died last week from some jungle rot virus. They are a classic old Brazil couple, him with tight curled white hair, hers is long and her eyes are direct. A painted Jesus, with his heart bared for our good, hangs on the wall, next to a recent photo of the couple. The hard packed dirt floor is swept clean. The place and the people remind me of the *curandeiro* Manoel Agosto and his wife, a fond memory of the man who cured my bad back 20 years ago in Pará. When we depart, I tell them I have travelled 12,000—and 2—kilometers to meet them. They are amused.

Now Marcio has topped off his tall pack with a back-breaking cylinder of gas for the stove. All supplies must be schlepped in on foot. The reasonable trail climbs and follows a course carved out by water. A bridge of enormous timbers, matched aside one and another, like you would find in a Japanese garden, traverses a swampy bit. We trudge on through a jungle of brushy trees festooned with vines and occasionally punctuated by red termite palaces (*cupinzeiros*). The heat is hot, but not particularly humid, which is a treat. Marcio calls for a rest and I tease him for hauling a 40 pound container just so he can have the chair to sit on. "*Sua cadeira*," I repeat and this time he deciphers my small joke. We hike on and on with two more breath-stops and *pertinho*, almost there. 300 meters more. A thatched one room adobe house sits quiet and dusty surrounded by jungle. The dried mud bricks are studded with crystals. We are in. Nothing to it. By the time my hammock is hung, it gets really dark. THAT is good timing.

At night more snakes, the *Caninana*, the *Sucuri*, come out, not to mention spiders, bats, and *onças*. And I cannot pass up the opportunity here for an etymological digression: The Portuguese for jaguar/panther is *onça* and finds a cognate—

"ounce"—in English as used by Shakespeare, for instance in *Midsummer Night's Dream*:

> What thou seest when thou dost wake,
> Do it for thy true-love take,
> Love and languish for his sake:
> Be it ounce, or cat, or bear,
> Pard, or boar with bristled hair,
> In thy eye that shall appear
> When thou wakest, it is thy dear.

"Ounce" came into English in the 15th century and disappeared from use by the 19th century. In 1658 it went this way: "Amongst barbarous writers this feline is called by the name of Ounce which I suppose to be a panther." The word was applied to various small or moderate sized feline beasts vaguely identified. The original was probably *lonce*, a French word for "lynx" and the "l" was confused with the article "the" and dropped, thus: *once,* and on to *onça* for Jaguar in Portuguese.

Back in the hammock I am safely suspended above the ground where the snakes would wind their wary way; but there is a shout from Marcio, who has gone off to check out the darkness. Marcos and I grab flashlights and walk gingerly after him. When the lights are doused, it is REALLY DARK. "Look there," says Marcio. Glimmers the size of bald Eisenhower dollars shine all over the forest floor. I think "Glow-worm." Nope. Try: phosphorescent mushrooms. Even in the rain, they gleam. I cannot help but ask, "Are they comestible?"

"I guess you could eat them, if you wanted your eyes to glow in the dark after you died."

*****

It is a Day dedicated to an unknown end. After a breakfast of coffee and *pao de queijo*, a biscuit permeated with cheese, we set out from the hut to visit the nearest waterfall at the *Gruta Secreta*—The Secret Grotto—to see what we can see. I wear borrowed boots, the Brazilian equivalent of Wellingtons, already proven to be good against water, ankle deep mud, and snake fangs.

Seu João's slack-humped cattle have beaten this trail before, so the going is easy enough, though muddy. The hillside is covered in rich green grasses. Up we go and up and up. The Rio Preto rumbles through rocky rapids below and a greened ridge of maybe 1500 feet rises above us. Cows cannot be bothered with the angle of this slope and we climb alongside a tumbling creek that pools up now and again amidst gigantic boulders. Here is a spot I could sling a hammock and spend the day, but we are drawn further up the watercourse cleared of brush by a flashflood or two. Off to our left is a round pool of clear water a yard wide. It is an "*olho de agua*," literally an "eye of water," a calm spring reflecting the forest canopy in its mirror-surface. No person has messed with the environs of the Secret Grotto, but torrential waters have. A boulder, freshly cracked in two by a calamitous fall from above, shows an unoxidized white interior banded with an ochre skin. Unseen, but definitely heard and sensed, is the thumping and whirring of falling water that lures us on, over and under limbs along a rocky sort of trail.

The waterfall itself cascades over a semi-circle of black rock a hundred feet above the tallest tree in the canyon. Veil upon veil upon veil of white water flails from the heights, bouncing and splashing from one ferned ledge to another to the beaten white rocks of the creek-bed below. This nameless waterfall surely outdoes the not-so-secret Hanging Gardens in Old Babylon. Mammoth tree trunks uprooted and tossed over the edge huddle in a jumble beneath the falls.

> here is a place
> where the wind begins
> stirred by plunging waters
> the water turns the air
> turning air beyond
> whirring as it whispers
> here is where
> the wind begins

Rain seamlessly joins the falling water of the waterfall and we dwell drenched in its extended range, washed thoroughly of all the grime that got us here. I set to work at the *Gruta* plying my trade as "Nature's Little Janitor," as the rude Louis Smart put it. There have been Years spent ankle-deep in Ozark streams, raking out mud and shoveling tons of gravel. During a session in the Kingdom of Kerry I was an acolyte at the shrine of St. Flynn, freeing the waters of his spring to cure the blindness of benighted souls, whether they believed it or not. More recently I swept off two years worth of detritus from the Grotto of Iemenja outside Goiania, ridding it of snakes and spiders, opening the channel of that great earthwork so its falls could run free to the Rio Caldas.

Now I put my gloves on and set myself to revealing the hidden wonders in this untended spot. All the while the water falls in plummeting sheets of white, amidst an ubiquitous rain. Just beyond the waterfall is a maze of bared brown roots over a small dark sand beach, an apt spot to gawk at the falls. After extricating wads of brown leaves, a giant root that is a giant's thigh wide is revealed as a living bench. Marcos tests it for all of us, as the greater weight contains the lesser weight, so to speak. It looks like a couch fit for the Pompidou center with its "springs" exposed.

A boulder draws me further on and I dig out the sand and rock along its edge and a teeny streamlet runs out from the earth along the newly excavated channel, a miniscule spring starts its course towards the ocean, in a micro-canyon suitable for a micro-gnome, whose existence is not generally denied around here.

On a whim, Marcos and I decide to follow the root bench to its source back into the wet woods. The root undulates like some Jurassic snake, big even by Amazon standards, and meanders over the ground for thirty yards or so before hooking into the trunk of an enormous finned tree that seems a cross between some mighty oak and an even mightier *samaumeira*. Its mossed column towers into the rain. With the huge tree for a landmark, we proceed further into the forest towards a rectangular boulder set like a table slightly tilted with the pitch of the hillside. It fell a thousand years ago with a tremendous thump whose echo probably reverberated into the 12th century. Marcos pokes around it, as the rain beats louder and the waterfall's roar increases. We will not be leaving any time soon, as the creek we crossed to get here is now impassable. We are sort of trapped, but can always go up the side of the ridge to escape any Class III Cataclysm. Marcio goes off to move our gear up the hill. There is plenty of tuning up to do where we are. I am glad I am wearing the borrowed boots.

On the other side of the boulder, Marcos' face lights up in the grey gloaming of the forest. "Touch this streamlet," he says. I do and I suppose my face lights up too. The water is warm. Not hot, but definitely warm. We have stumbled on a buried thermal spring. My leather gloves provide protection against thorns and the unlikely, but possible, presence of a viper, as I paw the dirt out from the crevices around the huge boulder, reaching under its lip to open the stanched fissures. The warm water runs faster, mollified by titanic pressures generated inside the earth's crust.

Marcos digs some more. Marcio, who has returned from saving our gear, rejoices in the discovery of the heretofore unknown spring. I circumambulate the site again and again, kicking a trail clear, then slosh my way down the tumbling warm tributary to clear its race to the unnamed creeklet that runs to the Rio Preto.

The rain has diminished. I sweep off the boulder, preparing an altar-like space, and arrange a few items from my leather medicine bag:

Three Chinese coins, with holes in their centers
One lead Minié ball from the American Civil War—1862
A miniscule leather pouch with Lord knows what inside
Three of the crystals fetched on the trail here
One emerald shard
One archaic arrowhead, 9000 years old,
   from Gourd Creek Cave
One not so archaic arrowhead, only 4000 years old,
   from Moonshine Hollow
One small bronze Buddha bought on a bridge in Beijing,
   a year and a day ago

In short order all these items are ordered in mandala-array. Marcos lights up a cigarette and walks around the boulder three times to smoke it, a practice approved by the

Sioux, if not the surgeon general. Marcio misunderstands my request that he drown—*afogar*—the Buddha in a sort of full immersion baptism in the warm waters of the spring. Instead, he buries—*enterrar*—the Buddha deep under the rock. Oh, well.

We each take turns tossing the coins in the manner of the *I Ching:* I get a "nine", Marcio a "nine", Marcos an "eight." Using an inspired shortcut that would either delight or confound Confucius that translates with changes factored in to:

The image for the hexagram of CONTEMPLATION is rendered by Missouri scholar-bard Bob Dyer as:

> from my roof on a ridge above the valley
> visible once more between the leaves
> i watch a thunderhead build in the Western
> sky and when i turn to face the East
> there is the Great Red Buddha's eye
> about to open

One more action: I pick out the emerald shard from the array, hand it to Marcos and advise him to throw it as far as he can. He gives me a strange look and then launches it towards the waterfall. Marcio and I toss some crystals away for good measure.

I am almost delirious with joy at the dirty dog dumb luck of our discovery. I wonder if the Indios Ava Canoeiros who lived here for millennia knew about this spring. Or perhaps it had recently worked its way to the surface. Ain't nobody knows.

Finally I make bold to name the spring, with the approval of my companions. I have been feeling the presence of my sweetheart back home, who so loves warm waters and us so rich in cold Ozark springs… I nominate: the Spring of Saint Mary of the Warm Waters (*Olho de Santa Maria das Aguas Mornas*)! A cheer happens to celebrate the opening of this "eye" of rare waters. Could these be the hot tears of the Mother of the World. I think not.

All we have to do now is rescue the Buried Buddha and we are done. I dig away in the water-warmed earth. No Buddha. Marcio's turn. No Buddha. Marcos. No Buddha. Either he is buried deeper or has washed downstream. No Buddha. I happily accept his escape out of the confines of my medicine bag to be interred in the domain of the *Olho de Santa Maria das Aguas Mornas*.

The Secret Grotto now has a new feature in the thermal spring. It is seeded with an emerald shard and crystals, larded with a buried Buddha, ringed with new trails, and outfitted with a natural bench. That ought to do it. The creek is down and we are free to slog back towards civilization, such as it is…

The heavy rain has washed the earth, raising a crop of crystals that paves the path through the woods. A few are pentagonal, but most look like busted glass at the recycling center, except they are clear crystals broken by the upheavals of the Earth. I get down on my knees on the sandy trail surfaced with crystals and fill my bag with the brute gems for whatever luck they might focus. At the literal least, such crystals draw music out of the heavens into primitive radios…

*****

The next day I resist the temptation to revisit the Secret Grotto and the Warm Spring of Santa Maria. Instead I choose a kind of stillness, suspended in a hammock by the shores of Rio Preto. I have tried to get Marcos to let me translate that as "Dark River," but he holds the literal ground with "Black River." The opaque crystalline water is strangely transparent when it pools up, but I am posted at a ninety degree bend at the foot of long rapid (*corredeira*) of tumbling waters that seem directed right at me but flinch at the last moment sluicing away to the north. In the Ozarks we often toy with newcomers to the

Big Piney River about the real dangers of Forty Foot Falls, which is famous for flipping just about everybody sooner or later. Around the bend you can hear it roaring, but when it comes in view, so does the trick: Forty Foot Falls is forty feet long and drops about three feet. This rapid now at my side we would call Four Hundred Foot Falls, and today—rain-thick—it is a Class IV Rapid with standing waves and wild whirlpools. In a kayak it would be a screamer, but in the hammock floating a foot above its surface I enjoy a cool sweet ride of stillness invulnerable to the relentless forces of liquid gravity racketing next to me.

The arms of a jungle tree supports the blue hammock. My view is up into the rolling rapids, then the smooth river, then precipitous hills hiding unknown waterfalls in slanted canyons obscured by green foliage that stops abruptly at the ridge line, giving way to a serious blue inhabited by ultra white mountains of clouds. Could I be content?

I close my eyes to dream awake. Nothing but river sounds until memory invades oblivion and I recall the time I figured out, not who I am, but at least where I was… It was somewhere up the Rio Negro—another "Black River—a bit north of Manaus where the dark tributary of the Amazon River combines with the major current in a turbulent confluence called the "Meeting of the Waters." Good fortune, caused by a severe lack of money, had sent me to a ½ star residence: a hut atop a raft anchored in a quiet backwash bordered by parrot-filled jungle.

Senhor Pedroso, *o dono da jangada* (raft boss) was a local who knew the woods and what lurked in the dark waters under us. For example, he knew where you could catch piranha to eat, using meat on a hook with a wire leader. He knew when it was okay to swim in the same fishing hole, that is when the river was up. It was up. Pedrinho, a Hindu-Brazilian, who had the English Senhor Pedroso lacked, helped out. Pedroso and I hit it off somehow, despite our mutual ignorance of each other's language. Gesture, expression, and attitude proved more meaningful than mere words. One *madrugada* he woke me up from snoring in my hammock and pointed at the wooden canoe lashed to the deck of the raft. I wedged myself in the stern and took the heavy wooden paddle with its diamond-shaped blade and guided us into the obscurity of the dark river. If there was a moon, I do not remember it. We both wore wide straw hats to ward off branches and the snakes and spiders that might be in them. He held a trident in one hand and in the other a flashlight, that tunneled a gleam into the gloom. I figured out that we were alligator hunting. It reminded me of a gigging expedition in the Ozarks, though the prey here was not the hogmolly, a toothless bottom feeder, but equatorial alligators. I was not actually interested in bagging an alligator, but I sure liked being out on the jungle river at night with someone who knew how to be there. Three times twin luminous balls of red reflected off the deep retinas of wary alligators. Three times Pedroso let fly the trident. Three times he missed—much to my relief and to his frustration. Eventually I paddled us back to the raft, him a bit sheepish and me wishing I knew how to say, "Better luck next time."

The next day they turned me loose in the canoe. Pedrinho cautioned me to be back before dark. I had some beers, a hammock, some rope, and my deerskin bag stuffed with power objects: Ozark arrowheads, emerald bits, a small statue of St. Anthony, a compass. I paddled upriver, spooking a flock of parrots that squawked off into the woods. I landed the canoe on a tiny beach of a small island. There were plenty of looming trees to choose from to tie up the blue cotton hammock given to me by the students back in Belém. Secured efficiently it was suspended in an arc that hovered above the forest floor. I lowered myself in at a 45 degree angle: An umbrella of leaves above, cumulating clouds above that, the occasional white heron poking around for a fish, the buzz of innumerable bees, the pleasant caress of warm wind.

I finally looked inside myself. To put it positively my life back home was a monument to the constructive process of ruin. The only choices I could see were between dissolution and destruction, a fine distinction that. My personal confusion was possibly terminal as far as I knew, which was not far. At that point I settled into the suspended stillness induced by the hammock. I oriented myself by pulling a small compass out of the deerskin medicine bag made for me by a Crow from Chicago.

> Head to the north
> Feet to the South
> Right arm stretched West
> Left arm stretched East
> My body, describing the cardinal points of the compass, was suspended on the belt of the Earth.
> My breath slowed and deepened.

The Sun burned a molten hole
   of white gold in the Zenith.

I reached down to the damp Earth,
   criss-crossed with viney grasses.

My eyes closed into a waking dream of emptiness
   filled with inescapable darkness.

Did I sleep?

When my eyes opened to the overhanging jungle, there I was fixed on the eight great directions:

      North
      South
      East
      West
      Up
      Down
      Within
      Without

I knew where I was and I did get back to the raft before dark, which brings me to the end of this memo-reverie and finds me alongside another black river twenty five years later. From where I am now, swaying in this different blue hammock beyond Upper Paradise, I can contemplate that still moment on the Rio Negro. I can see my subsequent travels into the world and through the creatively confusing jungle of my life. The Amazon absolved me of the past and laid on a navigational penance to coordinate myself, oriented by those eight great directions.

And of a sudden I realize something else: The warm trickle of the Spring of Santa Maria that we opened yesterday feeds the Rio Preto just above these rapids. The sinuous tree branch bobbing this moment along in the river will be carried mainly north to Lake Serra da Mesa, which will debouche into the Rio Maranhão, which will wander to the Rio Tocantins, which will pour itself into the mouth of the Great Amazon itself which is BOUND TO BELÉM, before it joins the Ocean of this World.

(Photo by Jorge Magaes)

INSIDE BELÉM

It is a "block party," the block being Mapará and the name of the party is *Mapará na cinza*—"Mapará in ashes." There are about a dozen people gathered under a red tiled car port, whose car has been exiled to the street to make room for the celebrants to dance away the collective post-carnival hangover. A *charanga,* a traditional small band outfitted with used up instruments, has been hired to counter the spell of a dull day, oppressed as it is by low hanging clouds such that it seems on the verge of sundown for hours. The party is a challenge to the fine grey ashes of Ash Wednesday, which faintly remind us of our own dust to dust trajectory, in this case mud to mud. And it rains. It rains all afternoon, sometimes in a drizzle, sometimes in a pour, but never quite reaching the deluge status of a *chuva pesada*. The relentless rain keeps the dedicated revelers in a concentrated group: drinkers and snackers and the three-guy band on the circumference, with the dancers in the middle on a cement floor. Across the street there is an endless soccer game happening on the field that occupies the center of the neighborhood. The kids are currently booting the ball around on a damp dirt surface.

Our party really is the last gasp of carnival since it is already the first Saturday in Lent. After a two-week celebration, which is supposed to end in the *madrugada* of Ash Wednesday, the six week fast of Lent really makes sense, is something of a blessed relief from the near interminable dancingshoutingboozingscrewinglaughingcryingsingingdancinboozingandallisdoneasIsaidbefore. The stamina involved is truly edifying and this cadre will not say, 'Die." I am privileged to join them, windmilling around in a merengue sweep sweep dance step designed to conserve buried energies. The dance floor is a *zona franca*, a free space where any style is accepted and the only prerequisite is the desire to dance. But clearly there are some experts here. Like the small woman in a bridal veil whose timing is as exquisite as her costume. Her husband has a pirate hat on his head, a bottle of cachaça in one hand. He sports a dark suit coat, yellow Bermudas, and a dog leash around his neck, which the wife occasionally yanks. Now he slings it over a beam and does a terrifying mime of the hanged man. Next week he will return to his day-job being a highly regarded pediatrician, known for bypassing the parents in favor of speaking directly with the kids. The music intensifies and I manage a few Michael Jackson moves without knocking over a table. My Les Blank *ALWAYS FOR PLEASURE* gold spangled pink t-shirt, a veteran of the T-Shirt film, emblazoned with a purple Wild Tchoupotoula brother in full headdress spins as I spin.

    Rain pours down but the tile roof, some cachaça, and the group warmth is an efficient insulation against the glowering elements. The 73-year-old grandmother of one of the kids splashing around the now sodden soccer field is literally kicking up her heels like teenager—for hours now. Later on she laments that she left her best moves on the island of Marajó last Tuesday and is having a few pains in her legs—but that does not stop her. Her husband is a white haired guy named Tadeus who dances occasionally with some restraint and prefers to sing off key alongside the band. Singing is also encouraged and again there is no prerequisite, like being able to carry a tune. And I note that just about everybody knows all the words to dozens of songs… The remote face of Manoel sings each song. He is a very serious fellow. He knows and sings *sotto voce* all the songs with quiet joy, including the broken hearted ones: *Tristeza não tem fim, / Felicidade sim*. "There is no end to sadness / There is an end to happiness." I do not know any of the songs. Even in English I only have a few: Two obscure Blake tunes and "Blowing in the Wind' and I cannot count on

"Blowing in the Wind." In Brazil lots of the people know lots of songs and they sing them without dropping a hat in restaurants, at parties, oftentimes with great style and subtlety, though this wet afternoon privileges joyous amateurs.

A *Nega Maluca* arrives, the stock character of a carnival-crazed girl.... The black face, the black body stocking, the curly wig may not be diversity-decorous, but sweet eyes shine out from the disguise and she joins the dance. A fellow in a technicolor shirt offers to sell me this slave (his wife) and I take the opportunity to come down on the side of *LIBERDADE,* in a loud speech, excoriating the culture of *ESCRAVIDÃO....* Slavery of any form: man to man, man to machine, woman to man and versa-vice is a state to be eluded, escaped, abolished. All the women in the group give me approving looks and truth be told my abolitionist pitch was a shameless play to that constituency. Then I say, "But in this case, I would make an exception." I lose all credibility and the lass, too.

The soccer field is puddling up and the kids use the pools tactically to stop the ball, pivot and pass. The dancers dance on and a young *morena* with Indian features joins in and her dynamic presence spurs on the circle of women to a rhythmic frenzy. The men have taken to the sidelines for the moment.

A guy with flashing sunglasses, lime-green lights blinking, plays the *surdo* drum. He keeps heavy time on the big drum with a muffled stick in one hand and a plain stick in the other which alternately hits a tinny cymbal. The boom di boom di boom punctuates the blaring trombone of the guy in the middle. The third member of this trio looks remotely like Charlie Parker and is playing an alto saxophone that could be one the master himself pawned for lack of smack. It even has a rubber band holding one of the valves to the bell, just like Bird's. He and the *trombonista* attempt to trade fours and trip over one another's lines. Improvisation has its trans-musical costs, but it all works together: the dancers, the band, the rain, the clouds.

Someone makes a daring suggestion: It is time to leave the charmed precinct of the carport and enter the greater world in parade around the quadrangle. The band gets up, and a dozen of us reach to the sky with ecstatic gestures and we march out into the light rain. These Protestants defy the church, defy the rain, defy the importunities of death for one more hour. The music blares and this group that could be transposed directly into a Fellini movie, dances around the block in measured procession, singing and twirling. More lent-observant, or just plain rain-leery neighbors, look out their windows. Mothers, holding their children, point and laugh at the grand testimonial, the last reverberation of carnival. The soccer players put their perpetual game on pause to gawk at their parents and grandparents and one itinerant gringo who dance in divine secular procession. Dust is now ankle deep mud, but the spirit of the Amazon keeps it moving. The pagan congregation completes the circumambulation of the block, returns to its shelter, releases the band with a generous tip, and proceeds to sing and to drum in a circle for a few more hours.

By sunset the soccer game looks more like water polo, as the entire surface of the field is under water, but the muddy game never stops, nor has the music, the dancing, or the drinking of this small party whose songs echo into the covering night. Later on I quiz my friend Moura on the nature of the day's events and he says off-handedly: "*Oh, uma coisa de Belém*—Just a Belém-thing."

ACKNOWLEDGEMENTS

The thankful receiver bears a plentiful harvest.
William Blake

This is an impossible task, as I am beholden to thousands of people for my fortuitous travels in Brazil. From ambassadors to streetwalkers, from cabbies to chancellors—with few exceptions—I have been treated with patience and with courtesy.

Eunice French and Professor Bobby Wixson signed the papers in Rolla that sent me to Belém where Antônio Vizeu and Nagib Matni arranged my first lectures for the Missouri-Pará Partnership. Gilda Chaves, head of the Department of Foreign Languages at the Federal University of Pará, looked after me during a Fulbright Lectureship in 1986. Branco Medeiros and his wife Clivia stashed me in their apartment during that time. The great Max Martins, Age de Carvalho, Maria Sylvia and Benedito Nunes surrounded me with big ideas and new words, like *putz-grilla*.

Diógenes Leal, who appeared first in the guise of a slide-projector operator, turned out to be a first class cinematographer, a canny body guard, and the truest of friends. Our quest for living images of the Amazon precipitated much of the material for this book.

In the early nineties through the Partners of the Americas, I received a Kellogg Fellowship in International Development, which put me in the company of forty dynamic individuals from all over both hemispheres. Under the direction of William Stedman, Barbara Bloch, Jaime Arias, and Emily DiCicco we spoke in three languages and merged diverse cultures as we pursued dreams and methodologies from Patagonia to Jackson Hole, from K Street to Tobago.

The family of Maria Jose and Antônio Moura, aided by the irrepressible Nana, has hosted me for weeks at a time in Belém. I feel like a naturalized citizen of their friendly neighborhood, the Almeida Bancrevea, where the guards at the gate let me in late at night when we would settle up our latest soccer bets. Walkyria Magno y Silva was a student of mine in 1986 and a big fan of Edgar Allan Poe. Now she is a highly respected professor and department chief with a Ph.D. earned in France. She invited me into her classes and, along with her husband Benjamin, treated me to many a dinner, many an afternoon of high-rent conversation, and a lot of beers. And the *companheiros* in Belém: Therezinha Lisiuex, Claudia Silveira, Gloria Caputo, Ana Maria Peixoto, Maria Helena Momensohn, Trabulo, Joachim Gomes, and MANY more. Film pals: Alan Kardec, Walério Duarte, Linda Chris, and Iuri Guedelha.

Marcos Borges and his family offered me a writer's retreat at their farm in the jungle outside Goiania, presided over by the most industrious Dona Gleide. I have spent days there deciphering my own execrable handwriting between bouts in a hammock and helping out with shucking corn for the making of *pamonha*. Then more time at the heavy cedarwood table was spent suffering with my miserable typing to get this manuscript legible.

The amazing Dr. Dr. Roberto Issler let me join a couple of his family vacations on the beach in the south of Brazil, for which I repaid him by teaching his sons how to play five and seven card stud. No wild cards.

Dr. Caetano Soraggi, the *Perfeito Prefeito* (the "Perfect Mayor") of our Fellows Group, and his family took care of me in São Paulo, coming and going. Every trip featured a last minute bulk hammock buy, for my return to the hammock poor United States. He also introduced me to the pleasures of old *cachaça*.

In Missouri I have been aided and abetted by chairs and chancellors at the Missouri University of Science & Technology, formerly the University of Missouri-Rolla, formerly formerly the Missouri School of Minds & Metallurgy. On my first trip to the Amazon I managed a complicated international long distance call to Dr. David Oakley, chair of the Department of Applied Arts and Cultural Studies, and said, "I sure could use another week here. I am learning so much from Professora Cerpinha!" He replied, "Take it. You are covered." Wayne Cogell, Dick Miller, Lance Haynes, Kent Wray, Martin Jischke, John Park, Gary Thomas, and Jack Carney all approved travel authorizations for me to continue my applied language studies and cultural investigations. Sue Kellems, Shelly Morgan, and Virginia Ostertag pushed all the paperwork along and watered my plants while I was gone. The staff at the Curtis Laws Wilson Library, especially the encyclopaedic Jamie MacInnes, fetched many a learned tome for me. Heroic student assistants, like Brian Matt, Max Tohline, and Lori Voss, guided me in the new technologies from near and far. The redoubtable Jerald "Jack" Brown devoted time and skills above and beyond the call of duty to turn drab text files into the meaningful maze of this book. Amy Waugh patiently facilitated the printing at Lightning Source Inc.

Readers of the manuscript included Fred Goss, Christiane Quinn, Anna Monders, Ryan Wylie, and the ferocious Bill Capotosto. Robert Stewart, the sturdy editor of *New Letters,* published several of the essays and the *Brazilogy* DVD. The core members of the Missouri Partners of the Americas encouraged me at every meeting, even though I was always late. Steve and Eliana Jeanetta, Eva Szekely—who let me carry her Stradivarius violin from one side of Belém to the other, Leroy Welchmeyer, Jo Ella Todd—who sang a Puccini aria in a canoe on the Gasconade River, John Henschke—who has three days seniority on me in Belém, Tom Titus, Jennifer Pilz, and Rita Witt. Clarence Wolfshohl guided me on the unbelievably long path to a finished book. Job could learn patience from Clarence. In the Washington office of the Partners of the Americas Carmen Sepassi, Michelle Nicholson, Matt Clausen, and Steve Vetter have been especially helpful.

Phillip Streamer customized the map of Brazil and hung the sliver moon in the black sky. Jesse Singleton in the S&T print shop came up with test copies. The astounding Bill Yeazel is to be found elsewhere in this volume by the close reader under the title of "Umbrellaman," and remains an exemplar of relentless travel, without fear and full of generosity. Tia Simone, Danilo Fernandes, and the Goes family kept me in Brazilian conversation and *feijao* back in Rolla during the late eighties.

I owe the penultimate paragraph of these acknowledgements to the cabdrivers of Brazil. Truth be told, I am not tough enough to negotiate the urban bus in Belém, or even in London. And besides I like sitting in the front seat—*com licença*—next to the driver and trying my luck with his particular accent, of which there are diverse in Pará. Usually the *motoristas* can understand me and I can understand them because we talk shop.

In my youth during the summer of '67, I drove a Checker cab in Chicago. I may have been the last Irishman to do so. Truth be told again, my mother did not permit me to drive after dark. She was wiser than I knew at the time. Anyway, our conversations center on working conditions, which usually mean for them 12 to 14 hours a day. I had topped out at 10 and my lower back could not take it, making the option of higher education even more alluring. My only consolation for my random tutors is to note their luck in not having to drive on ice or through drifts of snow. One time, however, Francisco had to maneuver us like a jet-ski with cresting wake through two feet of water that was running ACROSS the road during a tremendous equatorial downpour. Another time I got picked up by Antônio Barbosa e Silva, who I had not seen in ten years, since he and I were both regulars at the cab stand by the Hotel Regente. His two sons were now grown up. Although I have probably tipped more than I ever made as a cabbie, I have received countless good luck blessings validated with open smiles, the efficacy of which I have but little doubt.

    Ultimately, *minha Maria querida* always welcomed me back home in the Ozarks, which made setting out worth the risk.

                             James Bogan
                             Chacara Grande Bargem
                             Municipio Bela Vista
                             Goiás, Brasil
                             22 Fevereiro, 2011

BIO-BLURB

James Bogan is a professor of art history, a poet, and a filmmaker, who has taught at the Missouri University of Science & Technology since 1969. His scholarly publications include *Sparks of Fire* (1982), an experimental anthology on William Blake, and *Burden of Dreams* (1984), a casebook on Les Blank's film. In 1986 he lectured at the Federal University of Pará in Brazil as a Fulbright Fellow, where he also began his career as a documentary film-maker with *T-Shirt Cantata*. Since then he has made several more films about the Amazon including *The Hammock Variations* (1996) and *The Adventures of the Amazon Queen* (2007). *Tom Benton's Missouri* (1992), a half-hour documentary on the most ambitious mural of America's foremost muralist, won numerous awards including "Best Short Feature" at the Great Plains Film Festival. *NAKED BRONZE: Louis Smart Sculptor in the Ozarks* (2009) is another film that documents the artistic process. Bogan's prose and poetry have been published widely in magazines like *River Styx*, *New Letters,* and *Walking,* and several pieces have been aired on National Public Radio's *All Things Considered, The Savvy Traveler,* and *Market Place*. He was selected as a Kellogg Fellow for International Development in 1993 and participated in a leadership training program with 40 other Fellows from the United States and Latin America. *Ozark Meandering,* a book of maximal poetry and poetic prose, was letterset at Timberline Press in 1999, making it "the last handmade book of the twentieth century." In 1997 he was named a "Distinguished Teaching Professor" at S&T. In 2002 he was invited to construct a three-ton version of *The Celtic Double Spiral Space Centering Vehicle* at the European Garden of Fantastic Art in Belgium. These days he can be often be found in a kayak in the Ozarks, dreaming betimes of returning to Brazil, Ireland, and China.

Readers of *BOUND to BELÉM* are invited to view *Brazilogy: T-Shirt Cantata, The Adventures of the Amazon Queen,* and *Hammock Variations.* All three films can be downloaded free of charge from this link: http://www.boundtobelem.com
Additional works by the author accessible at mst.edu/~jbogan

For those who wish to purchase a DVD, it is available from University of Missouri Extension for $30.
Link: http://extension.missouri.edu/p/DVD21

To contact the author:
jbogan@mst.edu

****

Missouri Partners Publishing
Visit our website at:
http//:www.mo-Para.com

Partners of America
www.partners.net

The Partners of the Americas is an international organization of volunteers working to promote cultural, educational, business, scientific, and technical exchange programs between the United States and South America. Partners pairs states in the U.S. with counterpart states in South America. Using a "people to people" philosophy, the Missouri-Pará partnership actively works to share social and educational experience, vital resources, and the development of apt technologies for improved living. *BOUND TO BELÉM* grew out of such exchanges.

www.ingramcontent.com/pod-product-compliance
Lightning Source LLC
Chambersburg PA
CBHW070633160426
43194CB00009B/1448